Media Lost and Found

MEDIA

LOST

AND FOUND

ERIK BARNOUW

With a Foreword by
DEAN DUNCAN

FORDHAM UNIVERSITY PRESS
New York • 2001

"Historical Survey of Communications Breakthroughs" is reprinted from Gerald
Benjamin, ed., *The Communications Revolution in Politics* (New York: The Academy
of Political Science, 1982).

"Introducing the Doggie Bag into the Soviet Union" is from the Class Notes section
of the Princeton Alumni Weekly (5/20/98).

Communications and Media Studies, No. 4
ISSN 1522–385X

Library of Congress Cataloging-in-Publication Data

Barnouw, Erik, 1908–
    Media lost and found / Erik Barnouw ; with a foreword by Dean Duncan—
1st ed.
        p.   cm.—(Communications and media studies series ; no. 4)
    Includes bibliographical references.
    ISBN 0-8232-2098-2—ISBN 0-8232-2099-0 (pbk.)
    1. Mass Media.   I. Title.   II. Communications and media studies ; no. 4
P91.25.B37   2000
302.23—dc21   00-047614

Printed in the United States of America
01   02   03   04   05   5   4   3   2   1
First Edition

CONTENTS

FOREWORD

Erik Barnouw, the dean of American broadcast and media scholars and one of our most distinguished historians, has made a career of bringing together things that ordinarily remain apart. As a chronicler of increasingly polarized times—and of some of our most divisive subjects—he has had occasion to clearly define a number of these fundamental differences. At the same time, and for a long time now, his has been a calm and reasonable voice that has, at least by implication, illuminated possible middle grounds, suggesting courses by which we may navigate and perhaps eliminate some of the distances between us.

The present volume of miscellaneous writings constitutes both a continuation and a culmination of this work. Written over several decades, and treating an unusually wide range of subjects, *Media Lost and Found* touches on many of the concerns that have characterized Barnouw's writing over the years. As such, the book also suggests the possibility of, and even gives some prescriptions for, a number of timely reconciliations.

The first of these reconciliations relates to the apparent poles of survey and specialization in academic study, teaching, and learning, as well as to the sometime gulf that can separate professional and lay people. This book contains only the latest of a number of implicit statements that Barnouw has made on this important subject.

Though there are sometimes tensions between the needs and nature of the general and the specific, between initiates and neophytes, Barnouw has consistently demonstrated that such relationships need not be adversarial. He sees general inquiries and more specific investigations as two stages of the same process. In writing voluminously, effectively, and beautifully in both styles and for both constituencies, he has consistently reconciled the positions of those who enter all the way in, and those who only take—or have—the time to look on appreciatively from the threshold. In *Media Lost and Found* we find that, once again, Barnouw has elegantly considered both forests and trees and is uniquely able to speak to botanists and bouquet-pickers alike.

This idea of the two camps and their possible *rapprochement* is of more than just casual, or current, interest. Barnouw's father, Adriaan Barnouw, was an extremely distinguished scholar, especially celebrated for his many contributions to the study and understanding of his native Netherlands. He spoke of such sunderings in the introduction to his survey of Netherlandish poetry, *Coming After:* "A nation's poetry is a communing with itself. In its music and art it speaks to all the world. But the medium of poetry excludes the foreigner. It comes out of the native scene and has no range beyond the native scene. No other art is so exclusively national and inaccessible to the outsider. Interpreters are needed to admit the foreigner into the national intimacy."[1]

Clearly, such national realities still exist, but I wish to urge a more figurative notion of culture and poetry and barriers to our more intimate communion. It need hardly be pointed out that our world has become, through commerce and technology, much smaller. At the same time, it is difficult to dispute that we have also become much more economically and ideologically and disciplinarily balkanized.

If media now constitute a native scene to practically everyone, then the outlines of its landscape remain dangerously vague to most. It is difficult to deny that many of us are unaware of the implications of our media culture and of our relationship to it. If poetry can mean the use of heightened language to express complex thought, then I think it fair to adapt Adriaan Barnouw's statement and say that academics are perhaps the media poets who most richly commune between our self and our setting. But to take up the other side of Barnouw's statement, it can also justly be said that in many cases it is academic writing about media that has become most disastrously insular, excluding those who could most benefit from its insights.

Fortunately, there are certainly many scholars who resist this hierarchical, isolationist trend. For Erik Barnouw, accessibility has always been of the highest priority. However specialized or professional his teaching or his writing has been, he has always felt it important to remain comprehensible to the uninformed but willing reader, and not to throw up barriers before him or her. But such comprehensibility has never come at the expense of nuance or complexity. With this current book we see again that Barnouw's work challenges accessibly, and thus simultaneously makes demands of and lights the path for the lay reader. It also effortlessly mediates between that reader and the erudite professional, exposing the one to the wisdom and perspective of the dedicated scholar, reminding the other that she or he is not just working alone, nor just addressing colleagues.

Though he may be most acclaimed for his magisterial surveys (*Documentary* [1974], *Tube of Plenty* [1975], and the three-volume *History of Broadcasting in the United States* [1966, 1968, 1970]), most of the articles contained within this volume clearly demonstrate that Barnouw is as effective a miniaturist as he is at rendering the long view. And indeed, the facility and frequency with which he crosses from panorama to Dutch detail does demonstrate the interdependence of the survey and the specific. Generalizations are only justified through specific proofs, which never resonate as much as when they are applied to broader contexts. Specialization sharpens the beginner's relationship to the subject, as well as the teacher's relationship to that beginner. At the same time, fundamental discussions can calm and give perspective to the specialist. Media studies at the university level are in little danger of simplemindedness (unless it is in occasional simpleminded rejections of things that are not presently in fashion). But while academics list in the opposite direction and map the corresponding disciplinary landscape, it is well to remember that neophytes can easily get lost. And even the most experienced and intuitive of travelers can benefit by occasionally re-orienting themselves in relation to cardinal points and cardinal principles. As in so much else, Erik Barnouw demonstrates exemplary balance.

This balance can at least partly be ascribed to another, similar set of binaries that are harmoniously synthesized in Barnouw's work. If specialists and generalists within particular fields sometimes experience tension, then friction between fields can be even more heated. One reason is that initiates can be impatient with a newcomer's scholarly baby steps and the outwardly banal insights to which they lead. But baby steps are essential to the beginner; as one enters a new discipline, undue attention to that discipline's specialized cutting edges may obscure its more fundamental, if unexceptionable, roots. Clearly, without roots, connections that spring up are in danger of withering quickly away.

But it is not only the newcomer who needs to step back from

elitist or even excessively specialized sensibilities. Specialization's
inward look can mask the salutary effects of others' elementary investigations. The fact is that even received wisdom can be groundbreaking, when innovation occurs in new combinations of the received.
Some of the best of these new combinations come when a scholar
begins to wander.

As the most cursory glance at his various collections of notes, bibli-
ographies, and the table of contents of this book will attest, Erik
Barnouw is a man of remarkable range and reference. Because of his
wide reading, he is able to find the key, clarifying connections between diverse subjects. The result is real, unstrained coherence, notwithstanding apparent great gulfs in time and discipline and
geography. As he crosses these chronological and disciplinary bound-
aries, Barnouw illuminates unsuspected and undeniable links and
suggests to us that, in fact, all scholarship is one.

Of course, this is not in any way a justification for sloppiness,
sentimentality, or the denial of real difference. Barnouw certainly
documents his subjects' multifarious and sometimes cursed contradictions. But he does so with a refreshing lack of jaundice or preju-
dice and with a willingness to see and even to celebrate an affinity
when he sees it. André Bazin, the pioneering French film scholar,
once famously suggested that those who split film history and expression at the coming of sound in the late 1920s were, in fact, making a great error. For Bazin, it was not the coming of sound that
should divide periods, practices, and perceptions. He felt, rather,
that there was a continuity of sensibilities that actually and easily
leaped over that perceived dividing line, revealing abiding continui-
ties and basic truths.[2] We might well consider disciplinary bound-
aries in a similar light; affinity not only gets us over technological
and disciplinary bumps, but it reveals how secondary those bumps
may be.

What characterizes such affinity is a certain openness and a fidel-
ity to key questions, as well as a willingness to seek answers wherever
they may be found. Barnouw comes repeatedly back to these same
queries. What are the roots of media studies? What do these roots
say about the present state of the discipline? What does all this
mean for the future? If these questions lead him to a Dutch painter
and an obscure Utopian sect, if they take him through the traditions

of theatrical magic and up to the cutting edges of technology, then that is as it should be.

Media studies should naturally be interdisciplinary. The media arts are culminations of all their ancestral forms and styles, and the extent of their reach really demands a basic acknowledgment: every field of expression and study is native to them. There is a final binary opposition that finds effective synthesis in Barnouw's writing. This collection brings into particular focus the latent content that lies beneath every scholar's explicit communications. This more frequently effaced element relates to the close, even inextricable link between the historian's craft and the historian's life, between the objects of investigations and the historian's subjective, personal relations thereto.

It is possible here to move into dangerous territory. A certain distance and perspective in scholarship are virtues, and excessive personal investment can lead to rather dire distortions. Still, Barnouw's work in general suggests, and his writings in this book demonstrate, the realities of lineage and the salutary possibilities of a writer's being directly connected to and descended from the thing he or she investigates. For instance, Barnouw has elsewhere discussed how his Netherlands heritage has predisposed him to all sorts of genrelike, documentary investigations. In connection to the material in this book, he has also acknowledged that he wrote his history of American broadcasting in part because he himself had observed and lived through much of the material. "I had touched on it all at various points, so the idea of drawing a private line through history was very exciting to me."[3]

Though the *History of Broadcasting in the United States* is informed by that personal line, it is not indulged and remains safely in the background. In Barnouw's mature hands, that trilogy's personal elements led not to distortion and self-absorption, but to an authoritative rendering of the material. More recently, however, Barnouw has more pointedly acknowledged and even foregrounded the personal. In doing so, he has brought important ideas to helpful definition.

House with a Past (1992) was the first of Barnouw's books that actually begins with the personal reasons for his interest in the subject. The provenance of his little old stone house in Vermont fascinated him, and his investigations regarding it ultimately led him to the LDS Church archives in Salt Lake City. His discoveries there allowed him to uncover the origins of his house and, therefore, to understand and deepen his own association with it. Salt Lake, which boasts one of the world's largest repositories of genealogical information, is an apt setting for a shift in style that has continued to the present, from which we all might learn.

Genealogists and historians both know that there are innumerable lines of family and culture, of experience and ideology that condition and form us, and of which we are victims or beneficiaries. Hard digging that leads to the discovery and open disclosure of these determinants can elevate our writing and thinking and, ultimately, our living. So it is that in his autobiography, *Media Marathon* (1996), which is built openly on private experiences and personal incidents, Barnouw explicitly uncovers the lines leading to most of his major professional involvements, as well as to his most celebrated writings. In doing this he is not simply indulging himself. Throughout the book Barnouw demonstrates the difficult discipline of telling personal stories that turn outward, thereby revealing not just one person's experience but illuminating the field on which that experience occurred. In *Media Lost and Found* we see in the more casual juxtaposition of disparate statements this same effect. Barnouw's writing expertly extends personal lines into public discourse.

Speaking in documentary terms, this is a call to citizenship—which is to say that journalists and filmmakers and broadcasters, academics and teachers and students all convert private interest to positive public action, to the benefit of and with sincere concern for all.

All of this is not to say, of course, that intimacy must precede historical documentation. But Barnouw's work suggests more and more that it might do so, and that if we are not necessarily intimate, then we should certainly be sympathetic. It is that sympathy that has marked Barnouw's work, and most particularly his recent books. As with the autobiography, *Media Lost and Found* reflects his customary wide range, his customary calm enthusiasm, his customary modesty. Through the articles here collected we see, beneath overwhelming technological shifts and social chaos, the human factor. There is almost a picaresque sensibility too, as seemingly casual crossings lead to abiding relationships and emblematic events.

So we find in *Media Lost and Found* both erudition and accessibility, firm focus and exciting interdisciplinary exploration, the public and the personal. To highlight these crossovers and syntheses, this volume has been guided by a number of principles. First there is something of a doubly chronological order, a combination of history and indirect autobiography. This means that subjects treating the distant past will usually precede profiles of more recent vintage. It also means that some attention has been given to the chronological development of the writer himself. Throughout the book we find the younger Barnouw writing commissioned, for-hire pieces with the partially imposed or conventional styles that we might associate with such assignments. Then, gradually, we move to the more individual and autonomous voice to which we have become accustomed. It is interesting to note that, notwithstanding the various contexts out of which these pieces emerge, the same confident and reassuring tone attends them all.

In addition to these dual chronologies, the essays are arranged to emphasize certain emblematic ideas. In reading, we find that these ideas are introduced and developed and recapitulated in a way that not only tells us of Barnouw's preoccupations but also, as he would doubtless have it, in a manner that reveals key thematic threads woven right through the fabric of the century.

This collection begins with an exemplary bit of Barnouw writing. "In the Flaherty Way," a glimpse at the life and legacy of documentary film pioneer Robert Flaherty, is modest and eloquent and concise, and it very quickly introduces a number of central relationships that have emerged not only from Flaherty's work, but that remain at the core of documentary discourse and media discussions in general. We have seen, and we will see, that these relationships—between representation and reality, tradition and innovation, production and theory, an historian and history, intellectual fashion and the verities—have been repeatedly addressed in Barnouw's own work, and that his ability to reconcile such seemingly contradictory binaries is a key to that work's wide range and unity.

The Flaherty article is another effective piece of intellectual diplomacy. Robert Flaherty is a vivid and romantic figure, and he has tended to generate rather fierce advocacy and hostility in the documentary community. In his documentary history, Barnouw has given us a definitive account, both clear-eyed and affirmative, of Flaherty's contributions and complications. In this piece he avoids the hand-to-hand aspects of the contemporary Flaherty fray and in so doing does him, and us, a service. Barnouw shows us the real beauty and importance of Flaherty's original contributions. Then leaving the documentary specialists to debate (as they should) over particulars of good and ill, he helps us to see what is most true and relevant about the man and his legacy. Flaherty's continued and indisputable relevance is confirmed in those who've taken up his torch and kept laboring. Barnouw also, incidentally, reveals how he himself is an heir to that Flaherty way and how much his own work has honored and advanced it.

Here is another motif that recurs throughout this compilation. The Flaherty way, as inflected by Barnouw, means that in the midst of industry—publishing and academic industries too—there are still artisanal, or artistic, values to defend and maintain. It means that when we talk about a text or a person, we must also talk about deeper structures. It means that preconception must be avoided, or at least acknowledged, if our search for answers and connections is to be fully fruitful. It means that unique sensibilities, without coddling or romanticizing them, should be honored, and that we ought to pro-tect the dreamer and proliferate what's best about the dream.

All of these characteristics of the Flaherty way are strikingly pres-ent in the comparatively early essay "G.I. Guide to Holland" (1944). Here we learn, with the soldiers to whom this was originally ad-dressed, to look beyond the stereotypes and see the substance of a situation. As he discusses in *Media Marathon*, Barnouw is originally a Netherlander, and this is the only published piece in which he talks in such detail about his cultural origins, as well as suggesting his feelings about those origins. However, it will be some time before Barnouw will explicitly explore the personal in his writing. Here, pri-vate convictions are merely mobilized to more effectively accomplish a public purpose. Barnouw demonstrates how the Netherlandish sen-sibility is quietly and profoundly present in all Western culture and history. A small country's small forms lead us to consider a broad array of resonant things: mercantilism and the creation of the Euro-pean middle class, non-superpower colonialism, genre painting as it relates to the exaltation of the everyday, and the creative treatment of actuality.

This is propaganda, but it does not come at the expense of com-plexity or humanity. In terms of the history of documentary and propaganda, "G.I. Guide to Holland" bears fruitful comparison to Frank Capra's celebrated *Why We Fight* films, also produced during World War II for the U.S. War Department. But in his article, Barnouw counters Capra's fabled pugnacity with some of his own subtle tenderness. Documentary *aficionados* may associate this latter quality with the work of English wartime documentarist Humphrey Jennings, about whom Barnouw has also written a superlative profile. With this refreshing and, for the time, somewhat atypical tone, we see for the first time the conciliatory and leavening effect that this simultaneously American and international writer was to have.

As for relationship with an audience, we here find, fully formed, that authoritative, uncondescending, trustworthy voice now so familiar to us. We also find the weighty subject matter that makes that voice effective. In this piece a (future) scholar (not a politician or a movie star) tells a noisy, self-assured, and at least somewhat oblivious nation why it should pay attention to a quiet, unassuming, and extremely substantial state, which struggles and abides. These are things, manifest in individual lives or events, institutions or movements, that riddle Barnouw's later, more celebrated writing.

After the general view provided by the Holland piece, we take out a magnifying glass and look at something more specialized. In terms of subject chronology, "Torrentius and His Camera," with some of the material on Holland, reaches the furthest back of any in this book. It also resonates, subtly but resoundingly. Without forcing the issue, a study of an apparently obscure painter and his obscure convictions develops into a contemplation of media magic and manipulation, the ideological depths beneath apparently realistic surfaces, freedom and oppression and the deep draw of the blacklist, as well as the ways that progress can rise out of the ashes of failure.

Similar overtones ring out from the next essay, "The Fantasms of Andrew Oehler," which also reaches fairly far into the past. Once again, though, this is not merely a curio. Barnouw turns his attention here to the ancestry of current forms and conditions. Since this is the case, we can see how this obscure magician's life prefigures quite clearly and remarkably the modern creation of illusion and dreams by technologies that appear magical and appeal to our fantasies. Barnouw also makes some passing points about how dream factories can run afoul of the powers and sponsors that be; censorship and deeper suppressions often come out of nowhere, and they have always done so.

With "The Sintzenich Diaries," modern times begin, and the prehistories of cinema and media and propaganda enter into living memory. The story of a forgotten motion-picture cameraman demonstrates once again how a close look at surfaces can reveal great and unsuspected depths. Barnouw's 1981 book, *The Magician and the Cinema*, is about how stage magic was overtaken by industrialization and eclipsed by film. This article shows an even more portentous eclipse: in film, and in manufacture generally, artisanry and barnstorming—older modes of both making and selling—move to the margins as Taylorism takes over. All of the media writing that follows in this collection turns on this very point.

But the victory of mass production leaves some remainders for which we must still account. Since the big guys have irrevocably overcome, is there a way to maintain and preserve some of the good out of that which they've replaced? "The Sintzenich Diaries" contains a kind of double minutiae—not only the diary entries themselves but the life they reflect. "Snitch" is one of the little guys, a footnote in film history, and one that wouldn't seem to count for much. But the poignant details outlined here (see Mamie Sintzenich's inscription in the first of the diaries that she gives to her husband) and the interesting everyday accounts that we find are emblematic of larger truths. Like documentaries, this article reminds us how important it is to give a voice to the voiceless, and to remember how apparent banalities can, with the proper attention, be as weighty as conventional affairs of moment and consequence.

Where the Sintzenich article leaves us considering the events and implications of the past, "The Kaufman Saga: A Cold War Idyll" spins us into a time and place of furious revolutionary change. This story of the Kaufman brothers takes us through the Russian revolution and the spectacular artistic ferment that accompanied it. Denis (Dziga Vertov) and Mikhail, the older of the Kaufman brothers, are in their own way as important to documentary history as Robert Flaherty is. But this tale goes beyond the brilliant euphoria of Soviet film culture in the 1920s to powerfully document some of the deep travails that followed. The story of Mikhail and his younger brother (and great film artist in his own right) Boris is poignant and emblematic. Separated in 1917, and remaining so through the early 1970s, when the story related here takes place, the Kaufmans' saga reminds us of what can follow upon the youthful optimisms of individuals and regimes. Yet it also shows how travail can very often bring forth good things. Here is a chronicle of both cold war and *détente*, of fractious ideology and abiding fraternity. Barnouw's balance here is admirable; he presents to us another complex configuration of private enterprise and public consequence, and he manages to do justice to both sides.

With "The Place to Be," the author enters the scene, and another kind of 1920s flurry, himself. This little episode deals indirectly with the issues discussed in the Sintzenich piece, with Barnouw himself now becoming the apparent cog in the big machine. A young professional finds himself in the big swirling metropolis, a little overwhelmed to be responsible for weighty things and important people. However, as it turns out, the most significant thing, or at least the one that is most memorable and pleasing, is a small coincidence that puts weight and importance in their proper perspective.

Next we find that a few years have passed and that the young man at the center of the last piece is now writing, sympathetically and very sensitively, about youth and innovation and much more. "Radiator-Pipe Broadcasters" (1941) is a tremendously good and significant article. The United States is not far from World War II, and on the eve of an explosion of propaganda and realpolitik and manufactured consent, we find Barnouw holding forth on some first principles. Here, while being humorous and popular and accessible, he quietly advocates localized participatory democracy, delighting in and affirming the power of people to act and to change. He emphasizes the need to turn technology to humane ends and to the common good. He talks about the constancy of change and innovation and about the neutrality of the same; he also turns a droll eye toward possible misuse and abuse. He sets forth precedents and echoes and offers careful suggestions of how, based on what's gone before, we should proceed now. Again, we see how, from the start of his writing career, Barnouw's calm and reasonable authority creates in the reader a feeling of confidence and trust.

The next two articles, "Mr. Greenback Goes to Town" and "Kitty," are also from the 1940s. While in the Holland piece Barnouw modeled the best kind of propaganda, here we see the former advertiser utilizing another tone of the time, and of ours too. We have exaggeration and manipulation, sentiment and idealism, and we have a kind of selling. This archival material is strikingly distinct from much of the rest of this collection, and it reveals a voice that we wouldn't normally associate with Barnouw. It is rather a delightful voice too, but it masks certain shadows. These are communication techniques that have not always been used to enlighten and inform. These are sponsoring organizations—in this case, government, which inevitably brings to mind corporate sponsorship and media conglomerates—that we have come increasingly to mistrust. Barnouw himself has articulated some of these complications, as well as suggesting a very sensible and kindly attitude toward them.

> I have to remember that I worked for seven years in the advertising industry selling Barbasol, and worse than that. My first job was directing a program whose purpose was to get women to smoke, because in the 1920s very few women did so. The cigarette industry began to realize that if women could be persuaded to smoke, they would double the market. For the same reason, they are aiming at the young people now.
>
> I never worried about that at the time—all I was doing was putting on a program, and if we got a good review that was fine. And if the contract was renewed that was better. It was all part of the job, and whether it had long range meaning for the health of the nation never crossed my mind until later. (With regard to the criticism of others' shortcomings or misalliances) I remember that I share in these kinds of sins, and that I was not doing it in a malevolent spirit. In fact most of the people I knew in the advertising agency were very nice.[4]

Barnouw's frank admission and generous prescription gives pause to the naysayer in us, even leading us to consider our own unintentional culpabilities. Of course, it should be noted that if "Mr. Greenback" is advertising, it is advertising enlisted in a good cause. And, not incidentally, it is fair to point out that from this point in his career and on Barnouw will, like that eponymous dollar, be selflessly circulating in the public service.

In "Kitty" we find behind the pointed advocacy some important Barnouw preoccupations. Here is more evidence that history is found in personal voices and that apparently small things can very often be quite momentous. There is an interesting documentary parallel here, in that this is a kind of creative treatment of actuality (cf. John Grierson, the pioneering Scottish documentary producer and theorist) that serves to make a point for an organization. This is not toadying or shilling and has nothing to do with the charges that brought the U.S. Film Service (U.S. government–sponsored documentaries in the 1930s) down, and which still raise the hackles of people antipathetic to any kind of communication subsidy. "Kitty" is not just an advertisement for the ruling regime. Rather, this kind of documentation/propaganda makes good programs known and accessible for the constituents for whom they are intended.

If these last two selections don't exactly address the issues that we now usually associate with the postwar era, then "Columbia and the A-Bomb Film," an article written in 1982, fully apprises us of the dark and lingering realities of that period. As we read of the agonizing birth of Barnouw's groundbreaking documentary *Hiroshima-Nagasaki, August 1945*, we follow two sobering parallel narratives. First, we see the rising action of bureaucratic inertia, governmental duplicity, and broadcaster cowardice. Institution after institution, pledged to public service and proper disclosure of the things we should know, dithers and hems and blocks the production and distribution of this essential material. At the same time, we witness something that Barnouw surely did not intend to portray, but which emerges clearly anyway. That thing is the clear, inspiring, quiet heroism of all of the many collaborators on the project, our author included, who labored inexhaustibly until the truth came out. In this we see another manifestation of the Flaherty way, which in this case means that one finds some worthy task, does what is required to accomplish it, and then disseminates a record to encourage others to go and do likewise.

Clear, relevant scholarship is one of the best kinds of activism. Like the A-bomb material, our next essay, "The Zig-Zag Career of Radio Luxembourg," provides a powerful juxtaposition with and contrast to the from-the-trenches, unironic propaganda of "Mr. Greenback Goes to Town" and "Kitty." It also relates in important ways to the student-radio article. That piece portrays the radio phenomenon from a ground-zero, grassroots level. Here, the transmissions start to reach farther, and the complications deepen. Barnouw shows that underground radio is emblematic of a key shift in the American experience on a world stage, a shift that likewise took place in the more institutionalized media. With disinformation as the common ground, he traces the trajectory from the joyful exercise of free speech—the students—through moral justification and substantial consensus—Radio Luxembourg in World War II—to the quagmires of license and duplicity that followed that war's close. Something terrible and confounding separates the Corporal Tom Jones described here and U.S. relations with Castro. This terrible thing is at least partly related to the ways in which citizen initiative can get swallowed up and appropriated—not to mention perverted—by the people behind the closed doors.

This also brings us to an important neutrality that Barnouw has illustrated over and over again. He is not an ideologue, a preacher, nor even a propagandist, and his message is simple and salutary. Radio, television, film, and scholarly writing too are not good or bad until someone chooses to use them for good or ill, or receives their messages in the same spirit. "Trickery in the use of media is a two-edged weapon." Just as the media are neutral until used, so too can people convinced of the justice of their cause suddenly find themselves the bad guys.

These last articles trace a trajectory of innocence lost and scruples mislaid. "Historical Survey of Communications Breakthroughs" is this book's most technical, scholarly, and thoroughgoing statement, and it summarizes these ills very clearly. It also makes far-reaching and even prophetic connections, demonstrating how media issues can reach to the very heart of a democratic society. We have seen how Barnouw quietly praises and gently criticizes, but here is the magisterial voice of the authoritative media scholar, and of a good citizen besides.

Looking across the whole range of Barnouw's writing, we see another strong recurring pattern, which this miscellany reveals with special vividness. For every time that he documents troubling trends (as in these previous articles), Barnouw counters that caution with a portrait of someone or something better. "Lives of a Bengal Filmmaker" is an appreciation of Satyajit Ray, the great Indian filmmaker, artist, composer, and publisher. Ray, like Flaherty, and much more clearly than Flaherty, is simply and indisputably a great man. And this affectionate portrait of the great man does what Barnouw's portraits most always seem to do. This is not just uncritical auteurism, or the celebration of a single individual at the expense of context, complexity, and history. By concentrating on the particu-

lar—Ray—and on specific applications of the particular, the reso-
nances just accrue naturally, without any compulsory means.

Ray, and this profile of him, resonate in a number of exemplary
ways. They both trace a path from romance to reality. Barnouw considers, through Ray, how the eschewal of villainy confounds those in
search of easy answers, but how such complexity better represents
and honors our lives. He notes how the unmelodramatic Ray is more
of a social historian than a purveyor of popular pleasures. The link
here between writer and subject is obvious, and it also leads to one
of this collection's most valuable lessons, and one that is especially
relevant for scholars and students. If, as he suggests, Ray began with
mere book knowledge of his country, then his long dedication to his
art made book knowledge flesh. So too with the far-ranging Barnouw.
Scholarship and study, though they may at times go astray or border
on irrelevance, need not insulate us from real life and experience and
service. Approached with proper rigor, commitment, and care, they
may actually deepen all of these essential things. Referring to Ray,
Barnouw also summarizes his own work. Work quietly and well, and
good will follow.

Erik Barnouw has been doing this good work for a very long time
now. "Games," an article of recent vintage, demonstrates that our
author's clarity and authority remain undimmed, advancing age notwithstanding. Here, Barnouw demonstrates the complexity of the
situation at hand, but through his vast experience and the number
of positions he can sympathetically represent (cf. Ray's antipathy
toward villains), it all seems eminently graspable. Barnouw offers
calm, responsible solutions to the problems of current cultural warfare. This means that he outlines not only the hot topics—v-chip
vigilance or censorship, syphilis or AIDS—but also the forms and
devices (lobbying and special interest, license and repression)
through which this cultural content is represented. The conclusion
is simple: our attention, our patience, our plain participation are
always required. As it was at the beginning, so too at the end: Barnouw continues to be a good example.

This collection concludes with another concise, deceptively simple
statement. "Introducing the Doggie Bag into the Soviet Union" reflects and benefits from the increasingly personal tone that we have
remarked in Barnouw's later work. This one paragraph, really a tiny
epilogue, is of a piece with the rest and the best of this book. It is

elegant, self-deprecating, affectionate, and redolent of great depths below. In his writing and in his life, Barnouw has consistently modeled these very civilities. In doing so, he has encouraged us to look for and foster them in our own lives. And in doing all this so well, and for so long, he has come to convince us that we will actually find them.

DEAN DUNCAN
Department of Theatre and Media Arts
Brigham Young University

NOTES

1. *Coming After*, xiii.
2. From "The Evolution of the Language of Cinema," in *What Is Cinema?*, ed. Bazin, trans. Hugh Gray (Berkeley: University of California Press, 1967).
3. Private communication with the author.
4. Private communication with the author.

For Betty

Robert Flaherty on location. Courtesy of International Film
Seminars, Inc.

1

In the Flaherty Way: Memories of the Robert Flaherty Film Seminar

A HUNDRED OR SO DEVOTEES of documentary will meet August 6–12 at Wells College, Aurora, N.Y., for the fortieth Robert Flaherty Film Seminar. As a survivor of some of the earliest of these seminars I have been asked to help plan a few of the sessions, looking back to the seminar beginnings, and to Flaherty himself. The main parts of this year's meeting will be programmed by Somi Roy, formerly film coordinator for the Asia Society, who will present a selection of films by Asian and Asian-American film makers.

Many film makers from around the world have taken part in Flaherty Seminars. Joris Ivens, Henri Storck, Louis Malle, Agnes Varda, Jean Rouch, Mira Nair, Susumu Hani and many others have come to show and discuss their works. Numerous other participants have experienced the seminars as a turning point in their careers. I count myself among them.

The story began in 1955 when Frances Flaherty, Robert's widow and often collaborator, invited a group of cineasts to meet at the Flaherty farm in Dummerston, Vermont to look at films—by Flaherty and others—and to discuss the state of the medium. The hope that others would carry on "in the Flaherty way" by then dominated Frances Flaherty's life. The participants, stimulated by the give-and-take of the discussion, resolved to meet again in '56—then again in '57 and '58. I was not at the first gathering but was at the second and third, which included Satyajit Ray. Having just won the "best human document" award at the Cannes Festival for his *Pather Panjali*, Ray had come to the United States for its American premiere. Invited to Dummerston, he brought with him not only *Pather Panjali* but a test print of *Aparajito*, just completed but not yet released.

We saw both films that weekend and talked endlessly—about working methods, relationships, philosophy, equipment, finance.

In a sense, Ray's films epitomized what we were reaching for—work done not in an industry process but rather in an artisan tradition, by artists in control of what they were doing. Ray's success, like Flaherty's, challenged an establishment pattern. The Indian film industry, like Hollywood, had become huge and hugely organized, split into hierarchies and categories. Film people had become producers, directors, writers, editors, actors, composers, publicists—separated professionally and socially. Ray himself was not any one of these and was all of them. Like Flaherty, he was a "film maker"—a term constantly used in the Dummerston discussions. It was not an industry term: it had a rebel ring. The participants realized what it implied: not only independence but the blessings and burdens that went with it, ranging from endless fund-raising to distribution dilemmas. One could hardly talk about "film making" without talking about the structure of society.

Frances Flaherty and David Flaherty, Robert's brother, spearheaded arrangements for these first meetings. By the end of the decade an organization seemed necessary to carry them on. There was talk of forming a non-profit corporation to be called International Film Seminars, Inc. I was asked to head it as IFS's first president. At this time, I was supervisor of a group of Columbia University Courses dealing with film, radio and television—which may have been a leading factor in my appointment to IFS. I remained president for eight years. They proved to be an extraordinary education.

The first Dummerston meetings took place in a magic setting: the huge studio/projection room in the converted barn that had become the Flaherty home. It had a sweeping view of wooded Vermont hills. Nearby, across a field, was the Flaherty grave, topped by a boulder on which a brief inscription had been chiseled. There was a place for an additional inscription—for Frances. Also nearby was a disused chicken coop where outtakes from *Louisiana Story* were stored, perilously. One of the seminar participants would make, from this material, the valuable *Louisiana Story Study Film*, which won a showing at the Venice Film Festival. Within the house, in the upper reaches of the barn, were innumerable boxes of Flaherty papers and memorabilia, chronicling a lifetime. Frances decided to donate all this to IFS, and IFS deposited it at the Columbia University Library. Many scholars, over the years, have spent hours and days in Columbia's Rare Book and Manuscript Division, poring over the rich contents of the Flaherty Collection.

The future was always the focus of seminar discussions: the need for films not based on preconceptions, not founded on studio artifice, but more directly emerging from life itself. What would be needed—in equipment, in social institutions, in new ways of distribution—to move in that direction? Although such questions were the focus, the discussion tended to return again and again to Flaherty himself—he who, a lone visitor among the Inuit, enlisting their collaboration, had crafted one of the most enduring of all films.

The film moguls had been condescending about it when they first saw it. They were even sympathetic, sorry he had gone to all that trouble, up there in the north. But they assured him audiences preferred people in dress suits. Later, astonished at its success under the Pathe banner, Paramount had financed a Flaherty expedition to Samoa to bring back "another *Nanook*." *Moana* had won its share of praise but was not, in box office terms, another *Nanook*. Paramount's accountants said it lost money. It virtually ended Flaherty's relations with Hollywood, and determined the pattern of the rest of his career: a search for support elsewhere.

Many of those who met at Dummerston—Ricky Leacock, Helen van Dongen, Arnold Eagle, Virgil Thompson and others—had worked with Flaherty, and their talk became fascinating when they talked about him: his ways of working, his ebullience, his brilliance as raconteur, his periods of black despair, his love/hate relationship with Grierson, his awareness on location of every detail around him, the mystery of the Bob/Frances collaboration—he the hard drinker, the nomad; she the patrician, a bit puritanical. There were contradictions and mysteries, some of which seemed to reach into the mysteries of the film-making process. I learned much from the talk at Dummerston, just as I learned a lot later, at the Columbia library, browsing through the countless letters, contracts, menus, receipts and diaries in the Flaherty Collection.

Curiously, one strand of Flaherty's life became known to me not through these sources but through another much closer to home. It was a matter not mentioned in the biographies of Flaherty. It astonished me, and may interest others.

My father, Adriaan J. Barnouw, occupied a chair at Columbia

named the Queen Wilhelmina Professorship. His courses and lectures focused on the history, language, and culture of the Netherlands. He had never taken particular interest in film, but one day in
the 1950s, noting my growing interest in Flaherty, he said, "I knew
Bob Flaherty." This puzzled me. "In what connection?" I asked. He
seemed reluctant to talk about it, and I didn't pursue the matter.
But after his death in 1968, I found among his papers a thick file
marked FLAHERTY. To my amazement, it began with a ten-page,
single-spaced, carefully typed letter from Flaherty to my father,
dated September 29, 1926. This was followed by three years of correspondence and other documents, 1926–29, some of which was in
English, some in Dutch.

Flaherty had apparently learned that Father had visited Indonesia,
then known as the Netherlands East Indies. Flaherty explained that
he was determined to make a film in Bali, which seemed to him, in
its culture, ideal for a Flaherty film. "He was particularly attracted
by the fact that no missionaries were allowed there. This should obvi-
ate our working for months, as we did in Samoa, to get beneath the
veneer of missionary civilization."

Flaherty outlined, in the letter, a history of the making of *Nanook
of the North*, which he said had cost a total of US$53,000, provided
by Revillon Frères, and had already earned a world-wide gross of
US$251,000, which meant a profit for both Flaherty and Revillon.
The reactions from around the world were extraordinary. Flaherty
quoted several, beginning with England. *Daily Graphic:* "I saw yesterday a film which will make history. *Nanook of the North* is a motion picture unexampled in the history of the screen." *Sunday
Express:* "It is the most remarkable film ever shown in London."
He quoted similar comments about *Moana*, for which distribution
receipts were not yet available. Flaherty emphasized what these films
had done for world understanding of the Inuit and of the Samoans,
and what a film of this sort could also do for Bali. To make such a
film possible, he hoped Father could provide him with introductions
to officials both in Holland and the Indies, and letters of support
that might enable him to win the backing of steamship lines and
other possible sponsors.

The long series of letters that followed make clear that Father
complied, with success. Meanwhile Father received from Flaherty a
letter that began: "At last it seems certain that we are going to do

the Bali picture, or rather, it is going to be done as a collaboration between F. W. Murnau, whom you have undoubtedly heard of by reputation, the German director of *The Last Laugh* and *Sunrise*, and myself. He is disgusted and worn out by his work in Hollywood; he is leaving the American film scene for good and all, and departs on his yacht, with my brother David as companion, within three weeks." His yacht was named *The Bali*, and Bali was its destination. Flaherty would soon follow. Meanwhile, he would be grateful if Father would write letters of introduction for Murnau, similar to those already written for Flaherty. Father did so.

After this, there is only one short note, from Flaherty to Father, apparently scribbled in haste. "Much has happened since you kindly sent those letters of introduction to Mr. Murnau." Now there was a slight change of plans. "For certain economic reasons" they were heading for Tahiti and would make a film there first. The yacht was en route; Flaherty would follow, sailing from San Francisco. They had not given up on Bali; they would make that film later. "Bali is the Ultima Thule of our desires." That was the end of the three-year file.

In Tahiti the group made *Tabu*, more a Murnau than a Flaherty film. Soon after its completion Murnau died in an automobile accident. Nothing more was done about Bali. I added the correspondence to the Flaherty Collection at Columbia, and sent a copy of it to Frances. She wrote me: "I'm glad you found those letters . . . that dream of Bali . . . only one among so many!"

A street in the Netherlands, showing the canals and the distinctive architecture. (*Author's collection*)

2

G.I. Guide to Holland
(Excerpts)

HOLLAND VS. THE WATER

THE HISTORY OF HOLLAND, its character, and its present strategic importance are all in many ways related to the position of the country at the mouth of a number of converging rivers. To make clear why you're going there, and why it offers both advantages and disadvantages to mechanized warfare, you'll have to understand its geographic character.

Holland means *hollow land*. It literally *is* hollow.

The country is chiefly a low-lying delta region that centuries ago was sometimes under water, sometimes not. To the west of this region, the sea tended to throw up a barrier against itself; it raised a ridge of dunes. But this protection was like a Maginot Line. Look at the map and you can see how vicious seas could and did flank this line to north and south, tearing huge chunks from the land, and sweeping inland far beyond the ridge of dunes. The Zuider Zee is a relic of such a flanking invasion. Even when the region was not flooded by the sea, it might be flooded by the waters of swollen rivers: Rhine, Meuse, Scheldt, and others.

In spite of these hazards, primitive peoples settled there. Later Romans came, using it as an embarkation point to England. They may have taught local tribes about dikes. At any rate, dike-building began about then, and has gone on ever since. At first its purpose was *defense* against sea and rivers. But in late centuries Holland has taken the offensive, and won from the water many new areas. This *offensive* is still going on. The most recent peaceful conquest, which was going on while Hitler was screaming his way to power in Germany, was the reclamation of parts of the Zuider Zee. This was only the latest of a long series of similar projects that have enlarged the country chunk by chunk through the centuries.

When a certain area is to be dried up, it is first surrounded by a dike. Then the water within the dike is pumped out, with pumps that, in times past, were generally powered by windmills. When the land is laid bare, it is then criss-crossed with drainage ditches, needed to take care of rainfall and seepage. The pumping away of water from these ditches, into a drainage canal outside the dike, and from there to a river or to the sea, is a process that never stops. Henry Ford, when visiting Holland, once remarked that Holland ought to fill up its canals and make motor roads. If it did, the land would soon be flooded.

The dried up areas are called *polders*. Most of these polders are in the western part of the country, specifically in the provinces of North and South Holland. This hollow part of the Netherlands is below sea level. The dikes that are found elsewhere in the Netherlands have, as their only function, the protection of the land against overflowing of rivers. Along the North Sea, where the sand dunes present a natural protection against rising water, there is one low spot in this range of dunes northwest of the city of Alkmaar. The Dutch here built three parallel dikes which they called "Waker," "Dreamer," and "Sleeper," each of them to hold in succession the North Sea at bay.

Dikes are wider at bottom than at top. But the top is generally wide enough for a road, and is often paved for traffic. When walking or riding on a dike around a polder, you will nearly always see a canal to one side of the dike away from the polder, into which superfluous water that has been drained out of the polder is emptied. You can sometimes have the eerie experience of standing in the meadow of a polder and seeing just beyond the dike, the sail of a ship moving on a level higher than you.

Holland, then, is a land that lives on intimate terms with water. This has had many important effects on the country.

First, because of the rivers and sea, Holland is a fishing nation that, early in its history, supplied fish to much of Europe. In 1400, Hollanders learned how to cure herring so that it would keep, and could be sent great distances. This was one of Holland's first great sources of wealth.

Again because of sea and rivers, Holland became a trading nation, a land of ports and harbors where ocean and river routes meet. Helped by wealth made from the herring she became a great ship builder, and sent her seamen throughout the world in the interest of trade. Holland mariners have left Holland names in such remote places as Barents Sea, named after Barents, the explorer; Tasmania, after Abel Hanszoon Tasman; Cape Horn, after the old town of Hoorn, in Holland; and Hudson Bay and Hudson River, named after Hendrick Hudson, an Englishman who had been in the service of the Netherlands East Indies Company. Hollanders in those days set up trading ports in North and South America, Africa, and the East and West Indies. Even today, the Netherlands East and West Indies make Holland look like a pinpoint on the map.

Once more thanks to its rivers, Holland is a farming center. Its soil is rich in river mud and grows fine vegetables, as well as Holland's famous tulip bulbs, shipped throughout the world. Holland is also the homeland of the *Frisian* cow. Incidentally, Holland's rich, moist soil is also responsible for its extensive use of wooden shoes.

For mechanized warfare, the land is conveniently flat, but criss-crossed with dikes, canals and ditches. It also offers the hazard of a soil that can grow soggy with any breakdown of the drainage system. Worse, it is a land that, if conditions are right, can be flooded by a retreating enemy. The idea of calling on its old enemy, the sea, as an ally in wartime was first used by Holland in its eighty-year war against Spain. This was one of the most important periods in Holland's history, and one that it has often remembered during its days under the Nazis.

HOLLAND'S FIGHT FOR FREEDOM

In the sixteenth century Holland came to be ruled by Philip II, also King of Spain, who set himself to stamping out Protestantism in the Netherlands. In reply, Holland revolted under William the Silent. It had to fight eighty years to make that revolt stick. During this war, Hollanders drew up a document in which they stated that a sovereign was made for the benefit of his subjects, not the subjects for the benefit of the sovereign. It is hard to appreciate now how radical and bold that idea was in the sixteenth century. It was echoed two centuries later in America's Declaration of Independence, and even then it was radical.

In 1574, the city of Leiden was under siege by the Spanish armies. Cut off from all supplies, the townsmen lived on rats, mice, the grass in the streets, the leaves off the trees. Any schoolboy in Holland can tell you that when a minority wanted to surrender because of hunger, the major bared his right arm and said, "Eat that, before you talk of surrender." Leiden held out for a year.

Meanwhile, William the Silent cut the dikes near Rotterdam. By carrier pigeon he informed the Leideners, urging them to hold out. For weeks the people of Leiden watched from their walls, but nothing happened. The wind was from the east, and it held the sea back. Only a thin film of water was creeping northward over the land. Finally the wind changed, drove the sea water inland and northward. As it flooded the land Holland's navy of "sea-beggars" moved with it, smashing more dikes as they went. The Spanish armies, pursued by an ocean and a navy, fled. The navy brought Leiden herring and bread, and the townsmen ate. Every October 3 to this day, free herring and bread are given out on the stoop of the city hall in Leiden, in memory of the triumphal end of a siege. On the same day all the people of Leiden eat *hutspot*, a sort of beef stew, because that's what they found in the abandoned Spanish camp. The story of this siege illustrates that the flooding of the land is not as quick and easy as it sounds. Dikes must be opened in many places to flood a large area. And winds are an uncertain factor. The blitzkrieg pace of the Nazi conquest of Holland, and the use of parachute troops to seize strategic places, prevented successful use of this weapon by Holland's defenders.

The People and Their Way of Life

Homes of Holland

To you, everything in Holland will look small, miniature. Hollanders have never gone in much for bigness. Having no bignesses to boast of, they just don't revere bigness. There couldn't be skyscrapers in Holland anyway—they'd sink in the soggy soil. Yet with some ingenuity Dutch architects succeeded in building a twelve-story apartment house in one of the newer sections of Amsterdam, which is proudly referred to as "The Amsterdam Skyscraper." In Amsterdam every house is built on piles driven deep into the ground. The city stands on an underground forest of timber. You will be told the Royal Palace stands on 13,659 piles. To remember that number, take the days in the year, add a 1 before it, a 9 after it.

You'll find Hollanders restrained and intensely religious. They have enthusiasms, but they don't believe in showing them much. They won't tell you their life stories on a moment's notice. Their newspapers don't scream. When reporting crimes, they're almost the exact opposite of American newspapers. They may not even mention the names of the people involved. They'll just say: "Last night Mr. J. G. killed Mr. H. M. by stabbing him many times with a pocket knife. Mrs. J. G. was present." The papers don't want to embarrass anyone.

Instead of size and sensation, Holland goes in for neatness and cleanliness. It's no accident that the Hollander's word *schoon* means either clean or beautiful. In Holland you will never see, at least in peacetime, empty lots full of rubbish and tin cans, and you'll see practically no slums. You will see something you may never have seen: housewives literally scrubbing the sidewalks in front of their homes. Today, Nazi tanks in some towns pulverized Holland's brick-paved streets and turned them into mediaeval mud-holes. But you will probably still find in houses everywhere the pre-war neatness.

The wooden shoes used only by farmers—and by fishermen—are never worn inside the house. The shoes are left at the stoop as you enter; you go around the house in stocking feet. By the shoes at the stoop you can tell who's home. On Sundays, as a matter of gentility, leather shoes are worn to church. Kids hate the leather shoes and can't wait to get back into the wooden ones. But don't get the idea you'll find wooden shoes comfortable. Till your feet get used to them, they're agony. In city and town, leather shoes are customary. But leather has been almost unobtainable under the Nazis. There has been an increasing use of wooden shoes, and of leather shoes that clack along on wooden soles.

Boterhams

If you go to a meal in a home, you'll find the evening meal like a dinner at home. In peacetime it would be soup, meat, potatoes, vegetable, dessert. But breakfast and lunch you would find strange. These two meals consist largely of *boterhammen*. In peacetime, you'd find a basket with quantities of bread in the middle of the table. Everyone would take a slice of bread, lay it on his plate, butter it neatly. (Etiquette note: don't break the bread. Don't hold it in your hand as you butter. Leave it flat on the plate.) Having finished buttering, you have a *boterham*—bread with butter on it. Now the Hollander would debate what to put on his boterham. There might be, on the table, a dozen or more choices: cheese, ham, jams, honey, and patented preparations made especially to be eaten on boterhams, like vanilla shot, anispowder, and chocolate shot. Chocolate shot was sprinkled on boterhams in Holland long before it appeared on sundaes in America. Having made his choice, the Hollander spreads or sprinkles it carefully on his boterham, slices the boterham neatly in four slices, and eats. He generally does the lifting with his fingers, but if he's using company manners, or if his boterham is sticky, he might use knife and fork.

The Hollander, restrained and economical, often has family rules about boterhams. For instance, a rule that the children must eat the first boterham with nothing on it, and that the second must have something not sweet on it. But war has brought much stricter rules to the boterham meal: no butter, margarine on occasion, hardly any jams, no meat. The bread has grown strange and grey, so that people suspect it of having sawdust in it. Two slices for breakfast, two for lunch, has been about the rationed quantity. Holland's boterhammen, before the war, were made of grain from the United States.

Life in Wartime Holland

In peacetime, Hollanders are great coffee-drinkers. They call their lunch *Koffie-drinken*. But of course the pre-war coffee came from Java and other overseas sources. Here is an account, by a Hollander who escaped to England late in 1943, that tells what Holland is doing about its coffee shortage.

> I am sitting in a cafe somewhere in England . . . I'm drinking coffee, real coffee, and in front of me lies my third helping of apple pie . . . I think about home, about the coffee substitute of ground tulips with skim milk and half a tablet of saccharin. The apple pie makes me think of the cakes of tulip flour and the sticky filling of white beans and artificial sweetening. That's how it was for me, and that's how it still is for Mother and Sis, and for millions of others . . . It is late. Better go to bed. In Holland I would have been in a heavy slumber hours ago. Everyone is so tired, over there.

Another escapee tells what some Hollanders have been using for tobacco: dried beet leaves and tree leaves. Holland's tobacco came from the Indies and America.

Others tell of the shortage of wool and cotton, and perhaps most serious of all, the shortage of fuel. Holland has some peat bogs, very little coal or wood. In peace its homes were heated with anthracite from Wales.

Because the people of Holland have consistently cheered United Nations aviators as they passed overhead toward targets in Germany, the Nazis have taken revenge by looting homes in Holland of furniture, plumbing fixtures, and heating fixtures, for the restoration of German towns. You'll find a nation badly housed, clothed, and fed— cold and hungry, suffering from skin ailments, eye ailments, bad teeth.

Sports

Soccer is popular in Holland. Cricket, and various games resembling baseball are also played. But the most popular sports are water and ice sports.

Although the skating season is short, skating is the best-loved pastime in Holland. When the canals and ditches freeze over a whole new transportation network suddenly opens up. Hardy skaters go great distances from town to town, visiting spots they never reach in other seasons. Even three-year olds are put on the ice, with a kitchen chair to push around and hang onto. Next year they will not need the chair. In a few years they'll go on long trips.

In Friesland, in the northern part of the country, if you want to be counted a topflight skater, you'll have to prove it by going the "route of the eleven towns." It has to be done in one day. In Holland most skates are made of wood, with metal runners. They're strapped to your regular shoes, whether leather or wooden.

Holland has more bicycles per inhabitant than any other country. This is a means of transportation rather than a sport. Holland is, of course, ideal bicycling country.

Painting

The country is very proud of its art—especially its painting. Holland is the land of Rembrandt, Frans Hals, Van Gogh. Its golden age was the age of Rembrandt. In the *Rijksmuseum* in Amsterdam, one of Rembrandt's masterpieces, *The Nightwatch*, was awarded an entire room to itself. If you should find the picture still there, you will learn how a chattering crowd can become suddenly silent as they enter a room and find themselves in front of one of the great paintings of the world.

Holland is proud of the democratic tradition in its painting. Its masters did not go in much for filling huge canvases with scenes from mythology or ancient history—fat Venuses, nymphs, angels and conquerors. Rembrandt, son of a miller, and Hals, son of a linen weaver, saw the beauty of the common people around them and painted them and their life. These men were not court painters, but painters of the people. This runs through Holland's art.

Traditions

Democracy is a strong force in Holland's history. Don't let the fact that they have a Queen instead of a President fool you: they are every bit as free and liberty-loving as you. This has made her people feel always a strong kinship with America. She feels this particularly because of her share in America's beginnings. Although *Nieuw Amsterdam* has changed its name to New York, Holland's part in her story is recorded in many New York names: Brooklyn, named after *Breukelen*, in Holland; Harlem, named after *Haarlem*, in the heart of the tulip fields; the Bowery, originally *de boerderij*, the farm. There are also the family names: Van Rensselaer, Van Buren, Roosevelt. And in Holland you will often see flying a flag of orange, white and blue. That is the same flag that still flies over New York's City Hall.

Holland feels kinship with you not only because she founded New York, but also because she shares with you a tradition of tolerance and human liberty. William the Silent, from whom Holland's Queen Wilhelmina is descended, led the country's early fight for these ideals. He was a Catholic, but he stood for a Hollander's right to be Protestant or whatever else he chose. In the seventeenth century, an age of religious persecution, Holland became an asylum of the oppressed. Huguenots from France, Jews from Portugal, Walloons and Flemings from Belgium, English heretics like the Pilgrim Fathers, and Protestants from Germany, all found refuge in Holland and made it the sort of melting pot America became in later centuries. You'll find in Holland names that stem from all those lands. You'll find tolerance and a hatred of racism. When the Nazis started a mass deportation of Holland's Jews to Eastern Europe, prominent Hollanders went to the station to carry their luggage, and wept. They chalked on the walls, "Till you come back." What they meant was, till sanity and tolerance and humanity come back.

For those things they will welcome you.

IMPORTANT CITIES OF HOLLAND

Amsterdam (AHM-stur-dahm). Ancient city of many canals, a Venice of the North. A historic place with countless old buildings, many with the stepping-stone fronts so typical of Holland's old architecture. Amsterdam is Holland's capital, though The Hague (see below) is the seat of government.

Rotterdam (RAWT-ur-dahm). Modern commercial port city in pre-war days, third largest on the continent following Hamburg and Antwerp. Terminus of ocean and river shipping. Scene of desolation in the five-day war. Symbol of Holland's hatred of the Nazis.

Den Haag (dun HAAK). Holland's seat-of-government. We call it The Hague. A town of fine parks, trees, flowers. Comparatively unhurt in the five-day war. But the Nazis are reported to have cut a wide swath straight through the city, leveling countless homes, to make a super highway parallel to the coast—part of their defensive plan for invasion day.

Utrecht (EW-trekt). A university town.

Leiden (LAI-dun). Scene of the famous siege. Because it held out, it was offered a choice between: (a) tax exemption for all time; (b) a university. It chose the university, the oldest in Holland. The Pilgrim Fathers lived here while in Holland.

Haarlem (HAAR-lum). Beautiful garden town in the middle of the famous bulb-field area.

Delft (DELFT). Home of the famous Delft-ware, and Delft tiles. Burial place of Holland's "Father of the Fatherland," William the Silent.

Alkmaar (AHLK-maar). Fascinating cheese-market town, very photogenic.

3

Torrentius and His Camera

THE KNOWN FACTS about Johannes Torrentius can be briefly stated.

Born in Holland in 1589, he was a painter in the greatest age of Dutch art. A contemporary of Hals and Rembrandt, Torrentius produced works that were hailed as among the most brilliant. They were bought by collectors far and wide, including King Charles I of England.[1]

His work came in two sharply contrasting styles. He sometimes painted nudes, tending toward the scatalogical and irreverent. Many people considered them not only offensive but very crudely painted. His still lifes, on the other hand, won ecstatic praise from connoisseurs. The Swedish ambassador in The Hague, planning Dutch art purchases, sought advice from a leading engraver, Michel le Blon, who urged him to buy Torrentius still lifes. Le Blon wrote to the ambassador: "I know of nothing in the world that can compare with these works, which are believed by some of the principal masters, and not without reason, to be the work of magic . . . One sees nowhere any crust of paint, neither beginning nor end to the entire work. It seems to have been poured or blown upon the panel rather than painted."[2]

Constantijn Huygens, cosmopolitan litterateur and private secretary to the Prince of Orange, wrote memoirs in which he commented discerningly on the artists of his time. About Torrentius he wrote:

> As to his art, I find it difficult to restrain my use of words in asserting that he is, in my opinion, a miracle-worker in the depiction of lifeless objects, and that no one is likely to equal him in portraying accurately and beautifully glasses, things of pewter, earthenware, and iron so that, through the power of his art, they seem almost transparent, in a way that would have been thought impossible until now . . . Torrentius exasperates skeptics as they look in vain for any clue as to how he uses, in some bold manner, colors, oil, and if the gods desire it, his brushes.

According to Huygens, Torrentius had been heard to say that his gift had come to him suddenly by divine inspiration. Huygens expressed puzzlement that this inspiration should have fallen so far short in his painting of living people, ". . . for he is so disgracefully incapable of painting human beings and other living creatures that leading connoisseurs consider their attention wasted on that part of his work. . . ."[3]

Torrentius did everything in bravura style. His real name was Johan van der Beeck, meaning "of the brook." In latinizing it, he gave himself an aura of distinction and also transformed the brook into a torrent. The added intensity seemed to fit him. He dressed with dash and was followed everywhere by admirers. When he visited his barber, they were said to go along to help bring water, towels, comb, and curling tongs. He delighted his entourage with ribald and anti-clerical jests. He was said to have proposed a toast to the devil. He had married early, but his marriage soon broke up, and he subsequently lived a life that was described as dissolute. He was said to have boasted, on one occasion, that all the loose women of Holland paid him tribute. Asked how he painted his extraordinary still lifes, he gave cryptic, provocative answers. He did not paint these as other men painted, he said. Neither easel nor brush were used. He said that his panels lay flat on the floor and that as he worked, a musical sound would emerge from the panel, like that of a swarm of bees. He was once quoted as saying: "It isn't I who paint; I have another method for that." Once, at a party, he said he had to rush back to his studio, or there might be an explosion. He said he did not have to lock his studio, as the pungent odors kept people away.

All his still lifes were small. A painting owned by Charles I of England was described as follows in the catalog of the royal collection: "Item in a black ebony frame two Rhenish wine glasses wherein the reflexion of the steeple of Haarlem is observed, given to the king by Torrentius by the deceased Lord Dorchester's means. $7\frac{1}{2} \times 6$ inches."[4]

Torrentius infuriated some of his rivals; some charged him with using magic or sorcery. Even more he aroused the suspicion and anger of Holland's Calvinist elders. In 1623 they instigated an investigation of him. They charged heinous crimes against God and religion and hinted at collaboration with demonic forces. A campaign was launched to discredit him and to warn others not to associate with him, on the ground of his alleged dealings with the devil. In 1627 he was arrested by authorities of the city of Haarlem, where he lived and worked. Some of his paintings were seized—from Torrentius himself and from others—and apparently destroyed. Descriptions of some of these remain:

- A woman sitting somewhat oddly with her hand under her leg.
- A woman pissing in a man's ear.[5]

Brought to trial, Torrentius heard testimony on curious and cryptic remarks he had made over the years, all solemnly quoted as proof that he trafficked with the devil. He was convicted. The prosecution demanded that he be burned alive at the stake. In prison he was repeatedly tortured to force a confession of sorcery. Depositions by several torturers—four worked in relays—remain extant and make clear that he confessed to nothing and gave no information beyond what he had said in court. The defense was not allowed a final statement, on the ground that it would be unseemly for the public to hear a defense of one so infamously guilty. He was sentenced to twenty years in prison, probably the equivalent of a death sentence. The trial caused wide agitation. A committee of three painters, one of them Frans Hals, was allowed to visit him in jail; it reportedly found him in woeful condition from his torture. The Prince of Orange urged the city of Haarlem to release him so that he might go to some other city or country to pursue his art; Haarlem authorities declined.

Then a letter—in French—came from King Charles I of England to Frederik Hendrik, Prince of Orange:

Dear Cousin,

Having heard that one Torrentius, painter by profession, has for some years been in prison in Haarlem, sentenced by a court of justice in that city for some profanation or scandal committed against the name of religion . . . be assured that I do not seek to favor him as a challenge to the rigor of that sentence . . . which we trust was justly imposed for so enormous a crime; yet nevertheless, in view of the reputation he has won for his artistic talent, which it would be tragic to allow to be lost or to perish in prison, we are moved by the pleasure we have taken in the rare quality of his work to beg you . . . to pardon him and to send him to us . . . where we shall take care to keep him within the bounds of the duty he owes to religion . . . that we may employ him at this court in the exercise of his art.

At our Westminster Palace, 6 May 1630, w.g. Charles R.[6]

The Prince forwarded the letter to authorities in Haarlem. When they still declined to act, the Prince took matters into his own hands, sending an order direct to the Haarlem jailer to release Torrentius to the custody of the English ambassador, Sir Dudley Carleton. This was done, and Torrentius was quickly escorted to England. At Sir Dudley's suggestion, he took with him one of his early still lifes.

Thus Torrentius became in 1630 a court painter in the service of Charles I. Physically he seems to have been in bad shape. There appears to be no record of any work done in England. He never again produced any of the miraculous works that had made him famous. An English account speaks of him giving "more scandal than satisfaction."[7] In 1642 he returned to Holland, where he died two years later.

These facts about Torrentius, with detailed documentation from surviving judicial and other records, were assembled in 1909 by the Netherlands art historian A. Bredius, long associated with Amsterdam's Rijksmuseum and a specialist on the Age of Rembrandt. He published the assembled information in a booklet titled *Johannes Torrentius, Schilder (Johannes Torrentius, Painter)*. A thought-provoking revelation was that Bredius had been unable to find, anywhere in Europe, a work by Torrentius. Various obscene and irreverent works had apparently been destroyed at the time of the trial. But the still lifes too had vanished, a disappearance that seemed extraordinary in view of their celebrity and the high prices paid for them. Bredius expressed hope that some might turn up.

Far from closing the book on a mystery, the scholarly Bredius account proved only the beginning. Stimulating new research, the account set off speculations and inquiries of various kinds—technical, aesthetic, religious, political. The Torrentius story turned into a complex saga, a lens through which to view a turbulent age.

The booklet prompted an immediate anonymous letter in a Dutch newspaper, suggesting that Torrentius must have used the camera obscura. Perhaps he had even, long before others, found a way to preserve its image—i.e., had invented photography. The disappearance of his works might simply mean that he had failed to fix them permanently. They may have gradually blurred and been discarded. The small size of the pictures, and the choice of subject matter, seemed to support the photography idea. Torrentius must have needed long exposure periods, ruling out living subjects. With still lifes he could also keep his methods secret. And he obviously pursued chemical experiments.[8]

This letter was quickly followed by an article in a German periodical, *Photographische Korrespondenz,* by one A. P. H. Trivelli of Scheveningen, Holland, which made a surprising contribution. He pointed out that the Constantijn Huygens memoir that had been cited by Bredius, relative to the rare quality of the Torrentius still lifes, included a further passage about Torrentius that Bredius had not noted, a passage of unusual significance.[9]

In 1621 Huygens had visited England and made the acquaintance of an ingenious Holland-born experimenter, Cornelis Drebbel, who lived and worked in England and whose experiments were financed by funds supplied by King Charles. His experiments apparently ranged from optics to alchemy, and he was said to have invented a perpetual motion machine. Huygens's father warned his son against Drebbel, suggesting that Drebbel probably had dealings with the devil. But Constantijn Huygens passed off this warning and became fascinated with Drebbel. In Drebbel's workshop he had his first glimpse of a camera obscura. It was portable, box-shaped. It showed its images upside down, but the images enchanted Huygens, and he took such an instrument back to Holland from Drebbel's workshop.[10]

In Holland, as Huygens recounts in his memoir, he demonstrated the device at a gathering in his father's house, to the delight of all. Among those present was Torrentius. And it seemed to Huygens that Torrentius was so exaggerated in his expressions of amazement that Huygens concluded that Torrentius already knew the device and had acquired "especially by this means . . . that certain quality in his paintings which the general run of people ascribe to divine inspiration." Huygens mentioned an "astounding resemblance of Torrentius's pictures to these images. . . ."[11]

If Torrentius already knew and used the device, he may have been the first Dutch painter to do so. It had evolved from observations of much earlier times. Leonardo da Vinci (1452–1519) mentioned in his notebooks that if, on a bright day, a pinhole is made in one wall of a very dark room—*camera obscura*—images of the outside world will appear on an opposing surface in the room. The images would "present themselves in a reversed position, owing to the intersection of the rays." Giovanni Battista delta Porta, in a 1558 edition of his encyclopedic *Natural Magic*, uses similar language, with the picturesque detail that "people passing in the street will have their feet in the air." In an edition published some thirty years later he speaks vaguely of the use of lenses and mirrors to improve the image and asks: "Would you like to see this apparition set upright? This is very difficult, often attempted, but nobody has succeeded." By the seventeenth century this playful use of a darkened room had evolved into something quite different: a portable room that could be taken into the field and set up at any chosen site, for observation or study. A painter could enter the room—resembling a tent, but opaque—and copy or trace the received image. In 1611 the astronomer Kepler was described as having such a portable, tentlike room. There are also references to portable rooms constructed like sedan chairs.[12]

Such devices could help a painter solve problems of perspective, but were hardly convenient. Eventually a more truly portable "camera" came into existence in the form of a box with a translucent screen in one side, allowing the observer to study the image from outside instead of inside the "camera." It was such a device that Huygens found in Drebbel's workshop in 1621, and that Torrentius may have acquired even earlier.

But could Torrentius possibly, as some were suggesting in response to the Bredius booklet of 1909, have taken a further step, a chemical step, preserving the image? Among those who speculated, few believed this possible. Most assumed that he had focused the camera obscura image on a panel flat on the floor and applied paint mixtures—some formula of his own—over the image to reproduce as closely as possible its shapes and qualities. They assumed his mixtures had not stood the test of time.

These speculations were thrown into some confusion by an astonishing event of 1913. A Torrentius still life turned up. It was found in a Dutch grocery store, used as the lid for a vat of currants. Torrentius had signed and dated the work—1614. Details of the painting revealed it to be the picture that Torrentius had taken to England in 1630 to present to King Charles. The stamp of Charles I on the back of the panel identified it as part of the royal collection. How it had made its way back to Holland, and to a grocery store, no one could explain. But its authenticity was accepted. It hangs in the Rijksmuseum, the one extant work considered by authorities the creation of Johannes Torrentius. Why had it—and it alone—survived?[13]

The resurrected still life now provided a focus for inquiry. Brush markings were not in evidence. The subtlety of the shadows and reflections caused considerable amazement. It was noted that the reflections in the wine glass showed clearly—though the scale was minute—that the studio had leaded pane windows. The words of the song occasioned surprise. Instead of an ode to Bacchus, it was a warning against excesses.

> What goes beyond restrain
> Soon turns to unrestraint.

The arrangement of objects in a circular setting caused speculation. It seemed to some observers to represent Rosicrucian symbolism. The Rosicrucians were obsessed with circles, which could represent the heavens, perfection, eternity, wholeness, or inner unity. But what did Torrentius mean by his assemblage?[14]

The Rosicrucian connection gradually became the center of interest. For the secret, mysterious Rosicrucian brotherhood, a storm center in early seventeenth-century Europe, was said to have been especially strong in Holland, and Torrentius was considered its leading figure. Curiously, this was never mentioned in the trial. But accumulating evidence has suggested that this was indeed the key element in the decision of church authorities to move against him with crushing force. There were reasons for the trial that never appeared in the trial.

Until recently, the elusive Rosicrucians have been considered beneath the attention of serious scholars. But recent investigations, such as the 1972 study by Frances Yates, *The Rosicrucian Enlightenment*, have changed this. And it has helped provide a new focus for the Torrentius story.[15]

The Rosicrucians burst on the consciousness of Europe with dramatic suddenness in 1614. That year saw the publication in Germany of a manifesto whose title page read: "Universal and General Reformation of the whole wide world; together with the *Fama Fraternitas* of the Laudable Brotherhood of the Rose Cross, addressed to all the learned men and rulers of Europe; also a short statement contributed by Herr Haselmayer, for which he was seized by the Jesuits and put in irons on a Galley. Now put forth in print and communicated to all true hearts. Printed at Cassel by Wilhelm Wessel, 1614."[16]

This Rosicrucian proclamation, or *Fama*, had circulated in manuscript, but this was the first time anything about the Rosicrucians
had appeared in print. The *Fama* was followed by a second manifesto, known as the *Confessio*. Both were promptly translated from
German into other languages and caused excitement throughout
Europe—according to Frances Yates, "a frenzied interest . . . a river
of printed words." Scores of pamphlets were published during the
following half-dozen years, in several languages, praising the ideas of
the brotherhood and expressing interest in joining their wondrous
work. Some of the authors said they had not yet succeeded in making
contact with the brothers, but hoped to do so. The brothers seemed
to be elusive.[17]

The manifestos ascribed the origin of the Rosicrucian movement
to one Christian Rosenkreutz, whose name incorporates the linked
Rosicrucian symbols of the rose and the cross. Today he is considered
a mythical figure, since no historic evidence of his existence has
turned up; but the account of him in the manifestos was accepted
at the time they were published. According to that account, he was
born in the fourteenth century of a noble but impoverished German
family and raised in a convent. At sixteen he embarked on a pilgrim-
age to the Holy Land. But during the journey, in Damascus and
elsewhere, he became aware of the scientific knowledge and age-old
wisdom of the Arabs, which gave his life a new direction. He traveled
throughout the Arab world, all the way to Fez, and was impressed by
the way its sages shared their knowledge and findings with each
other. Returning via Spain to the European world, he wanted to win
its savants to a similar sharing. They tended to hoard their secrets.
In view of the rapidly accumulating knowledge about the world and
the mysteries of nature, Rosenkreutz proclaimed that a sharing of
knowledge would soon bring mankind to a more glorious life on
earth. This apocalyptic sense of being on the verge of great changes
in the condition of man apparently communicated itself to many
readers, who must have included a spectrum of scientists/alchemists,
astronomers/astrologers, physicians/quacks, and diverse scholars and
mystics. Some rulers also took notice.

In Rosicrucian symbolism the cross apparently represented a pious
dedication to the envisioned earthly salvation—not to religious hierarchies that had become an obstacle to research. The rose represented the unfolding of the secrets of nature.

Rosenkreutz was said to have enjoined his followers not to wear distinguishing dress. Wherever they went, they were to dress like others in that place. They were to use their knowledge everywhere to heal the sick, always gratis. The movement was to maintain secrecy for a hundred years.[18]

That it should be secret, and given to cryptic communication, was perhaps inevitable at a time when heretical experimenters and thinkers were being imprisoned or burned at the stake in substantial numbers. At the same time, the secrecy and mystery fed rumor and suspicion, eventually providing the basis for counterattack.

Much about the Rosicrucian movement remains an impenetrable mystery. Were the manifestos that started the hubbub a description of an organization in actual existence? So almost everyone assumed. Or were they perhaps, as Frances Yates had suggested, intended as a call to form an organization? Whatever the truth, Yates feels that the resulting ferment did stimulate communication and meetings among scholars and experimenters "in the Rosicrucian spirit." Perhaps the manifestos actually created, almost overnight, a Rosicrucian movement. If so, this seems to have happened with intensity in Holland.[19]

"There is no country in the world," wrote a French writer of the time, Sorbière, "more suitable than Holland for the Brotherhood of the Rose Cross, and where those who have the secret of the great work have more freedom."[20] All this seems to have unnerved the Dutch Calvinist hierarchy, as it did religious establishments elsewhere. The Rosicrucians seemed to have forgotten about heaven and hell.

Wide religious counterattacks on the Rosicrucians commenced in Paris in 1623 in a publication titled *Horrible Pacts Made Between the Devil and the Pretended Invisible Ones.* In this their secrecy was pictured as a sharing of diabolical secrets. The rule against distinguishing dress was pictured as a sinister infiltration tactic. The piety of the movement was described as devil worship. Similar attacks erupted in Holland, where a 1624 publication asserted that "they conclude abominable pacts with Satan; they are instantly transported from one place to another; they make themselves invisible; they read plants, and can tell the secrets of human thoughts."[21]

The Calvinists were meanwhile urging an official investigation of the Rosicrucians. They enlisted the aid of the theological faculty of

Leyden University, which concurred that the sect was "greatly in error and heretical, harmful to the Republic, rebellious, and full of deceit." Pressure was brought on the city of Haarlem for legal action. A memorandum presented to Haarlem authorities stated: "As we have learned . . . certain persons who call themselves the Brothers of the Rose-Cross and who have had their residence in the city of Paris have now come also into these provinces, and are engaged in activities very harmful to the interests of the State. . . ." The memorandum said that meetings of the sect were found to have been held in various cities including Haarlem. It then mentioned "a certain Torrentius who is said to be one of the foremost of this sect." It was this memorandum that launched the campaign against Torrentius.[22]

If the Rosicrucian connection was never mentioned in the trial, or in the prosecutor's final summation, there was a reason. The Rosicrucians apparently had support among intellectuals and well-to-do patricians. One document in the prosecution file suggests that there were meetings of Rosicrucian members in the palace of the Prince of Orange himself. The Calvinist leaders dared not attack this elite directly and chose to move against the sect obliquely by discrediting the individual most prominently mentioned in connection with it, a man whose mysterious activities and pronouncements made him a ready target for the charge of sorcery. His trial became, in effect, a historic show trial, comparable to other such trials. The real target was neither Torrentius nor his method of painting, but a heretical movement.

Holland's judicial procedure did not at this time call for testimony and cross-examination in court. Instead, both prosecution and defense arranged for witnesses to appear before magistrates in their places of abode and give testimony there. This was all written down. Those mentioned might be called and questioned for further information or corroboration. The resulting depositions could be used selectively in the trial for arguments pro and con. The voluminous depositions in the Torrentius case, a case that became a *cause célèbre* accompanied by wild public excitement and alarm, have been preserved in the Haarlem archives and were extensively quoted by Bredius and by later commentators.

The archives make clear the determination of religious and civil authorities to blacken and convict Torrentius. In the city of Delft an innkeeper and his wife, at whose place Torrentius had sometimes stayed, were called for testimony. When questioned they spoke of a particular evening, several years earlier, when Torrentius in the company of other guests had ridiculed various stories in the Bible, spoken countless blasphemies, and even scoffed at the story of the Passion, until the innkeeper put a stop to it, telling Torrentius: "Shame on you! If this were Spain they would burn you alive at the stake!" Asked to mention others present, they mentioned the names of two other guests. When these were later summoned to testify, they remembered an evening when Torrentius had twitted the innkeeper on various matters, but they recalled no mention whatever of the Bible. The innkeeper and his wife were called back and questioned further, and finally confessed that their statements had been false. They had merely tried to be helpful to the authorities. They said the Haarlem prosecutor and another official, along with two Calvinist ministers, had visited them at the inn and explained how dangerous Torrentius was. They had given her a paper on which was written the sort of testimony that was needed. The wife had memorized it.[23]

To support the charge that Torrentius was in league with the devil, the prosecution relied heavily on the testimony of one Dr. Jacob Hogenheym. He and Torrentius had on several occasions taken walks together; Torrentius apparently enjoyed mystifying the doctor. On one walk they passed a boy, who greeted Torrentius effusively but ignored the doctor. The doctor commented on this. Torrentius replied: "That boy has an evil spirit."

The doctor found this remark thought-provoking. How could Torrentius know that someone was possessed of an evil spirit unless he himself dealt with evil spirits? Besides, Torrentius had used the same phrase on several occasions.

On one walk they came to a farm, where a man spoke to Torrentius: "You want a hen, don't you? I know you need them!" Hogenheym was puzzled. "How would that fellow know you needed a hen?" Torrentius said: "That man is possessed of an evil spirit."[24]

When Torrentius, after his arrest, was confronted with the doctor's testimony, he explained about his need for hens. He said that he sometimes mixed his colors in an empty eggshell, resealed it, and had a hen sit on it for as long as three weeks, to keep the mixture at a steady warmth until it was just right. The explanation suggests a sophisticated technician. Torrentius apparently explained nothing further about his techniques.[25]

As a show trial, the action against Torrentius appears to have been an unqualified success. It virtually snuffed out the Rosicrucian movement in the Netherlands and helped to weaken it elsewhere. There is little evidence of a Dutch Rosicrucian movement in the following years. Copies of the Dutch translation of the *Fama* disappeared. Apparently no copy now remains in existence. After the trial, Prince Frederik Hendrik seems to have given his protection to the Freemasons rather than the Brothers of the Rose Cross. Here and in England, a strengthened Freemason movement seemed to rise from the Rosicrucian crisis. In France, too, the movement seemed to vanish. Descartes, who had been rumored to be a Rosicrucian, made a point of denying that he had ever been a member of the brotherhood. To make clear he was not one of the *invisibles*, he made himself widely visible in Paris.

In many ways, the world of Johannes Torrentius had been a microcosm of the era. Microcosm—a favorite word of the Rosicrucians. To them, every human being was *microcosmus*.

The role of Torrentius as a Rosicrucian, member of a knowledge-sharing brotherhood, may help to explain his early acquisition of the camera obscura. Whatever his use of the camera, it also touched a central theme of Renaissance art. It was a time when painters became obsessed with perspective, and with that kind of realism we can now call photographic—an obsession unquestionably aided and abetted by the evolving camera obscura.

Its evolution was also a story of science, a field still hedged by perils. In the public mind it was still so closely linked to necromancy that probes into the nature of things were risky, bringing some to prison, others to the stake.

The role of Charles I in the Torrentius case raises interesting questions. He had a sister, the Princess Elizabeth, who in 1613 married a German prince from the Palatinate, named Frederick. This couple became, for a brief season, 1619–1620, King and Queen of Bohemia, reigning from Prague. There they were said to be among the crowned heads who were receptive to Rosicrucian ideas. When they were overthrown, with the king defeated in battle by Counter-Reformation forces, they fled to Holland. The young couple became popular among its social elite. They are mentioned here and there in the journal of Constantijn Huygens. For many years Elizabeth, Queen of Bohemia in exile, held court in The Hague.[26]

Was King Charles I's rescue of Johannes Torrentius in any way related to Elizabeth's espousal of the Rosicrucian brotherhood? There is no evidence of it. Yet it is possible, perhaps even likely.

Even more interesting questions revolve around Constantijn Huygens. Was he among those involved in Rosicrucian gatherings in the palace of the Prince of Orange himself? Again, no answer is available. But the story of the Huygens family reflects dramatically the seventeenth-century transition in scientific research. The father of Constantijn Huygens, Christiaan Huygens the elder, feared that his son's scientific inquisitiveness would lead to involvement with the devil. Constantijn passed off these fears but witnessed the destruction of Torrentius amid similar terrors. No such fears would hound the career of Christiaan Huygens the younger (1629–1695), son of Constantijn. Born during the time Torrentius was experiencing prison and torture, this Christiaan Huygens would do his work in another kind of age. He would perfect his lenses and his telescope, freely probe the heavens, unravel planetary mysteries, and contribute to knowledge on earth with the magic lantern, the pendulum clock, the spiral watchspring, and other wonders. So science made its transition.

Amid the transition lived the hapless, brilliant, flamboyant Torrentius. It was a violent and devil-haunted time—a time when, as Frances Yates put it, "the Renaissance disappears into convulsions of witchhunting and wars, to emerge in the years to come—when these horrors were overcome—as enlightenment."[27]

NOTES

Translations from non-English sources are by the author unless otherwise indicated.

1. Our summary is based mainly on Abraham Bredius, *Johannes Torrentius, Schilder, 1589–1644* (The Hague: Nijhoff, 1909). In Dutch. Other sources as noted.

2. Ibid., pp. 6–7.

3. Huygens wrote his memoirs in Latin. They did not see publication until the late nineteenth century, when fragments of the text along with Dutch translations appeared in the bimonthly periodical *OudHolland*, IX, 1891. Bredius quoted from this source. A major compilation of passages

from the memoirs, with annotations by A. H. Kan, was published under the title *De Jeugd van Constantijn Huygens: door hemzelf beschreven* (*The Youth of Constantijn Huygens, described by himself.* Rotterdam and Antwerp: Donker, 1946). The book contains a valuable appendix on Torrentius.

4. Bredius, op. cit., p. 10, quoted from Public Records Office, London.

5. Ibid., p. 9.

6. The French text can be found in Bredius, pp. 60–61; or in A. J. Rehorst, *Torrentius* (Rotterdam: Brusse, 1939), pp. 226–27.

7. Horace Walpole, *Anecdotes of Painting in England*, vol. 2 (London, 1828), p. 242.

8. *Het Vaderland*, Oct. 31, 1909. In Dutch.

9. A. P. H. Trivelli, "Johannes Torrentius 1589–1644," in *Photographische Korrespondenz*, No. 47, 1910, pp. 1–8. In German.

10. Rosalie L. Colie, *"Some Thankfulnesse to Constantine": a study of English influence upon the early works of Constantijn Huygens* (The Hague: Nijhoff, 1956), includes a valuable passage on Cornelis Drebbel and Huygens's fascination with him. See pp. 92–110.

11. A. H. Kan, ed., op. cit., pp. 86–87.

12. Quotations are from Georges Potoniée, *The History of the Discovery of Photography*, translation from the French by Edward Epstean (New York: Arno, 1973), pp. 8, 11. For the evolving forms of the portable camera obscura, see also Helmut Gernsheim with Alison Gernsheim, *The History of Photography* (New York: Oxford, 1955).

13. Abraham Bredius, "Johannes Symonsz. Torrentius: een nalezing," in *Oud-Holland*, 1917. pp. 219–23.

14. Rehorst, op. cit., provides the most massive compilation of Torrentius documents, with emphasis on the Rosicrucian connection. Some far-fetched inferences.

15. Frances A. Yates, *The Rosicrucian Enlightenment* (London and Boston: Routledge & Kegan Paul, 1972).

16. English translations of the Rosicrucian manifestos and related documents appear in Arthur E. Wait, *The Real History of the Rosicrucians* (London, 1887), and Yates, op. cit.

17. Yates, op. cit., pp. 48–49.

18. For a history of the movement, see especially Frans Wittemans, *A New and Authentic History of the Rosicrucians*, translated from the Dutch by Francis Graem Davis (Chicago: Aries, 1938).

19. Yates, op. cit., pp. 91–102.

20. Wittemans, op. cit., pp. 50–54.

21. Ibid., p. 38, quoted from *Wassenaers Historisch Verhaal*, 1624.

22. Rehorst, op. cit.. pp. 17–19.

23. Ibid.. pp. 31–36.

24. Ibid.. pp. 25–28.

25. Ibid.. p. 41.

26. A detailed account of the "winter King and Queen of Bohemia" is in Yates, op. cit., pp. 1–29.

27. Ibid., p. 224.

A depiction of rear projection, from *Le Magasin Pittoresque* of 1849.

4

The Fantasms of
Andrew Oehler

ANDREW OEHLER goes down in history as the writer of the first book
on magic published in the United States.[1] He published it himself,
in 1811 in Trenton, N.J., and it bore the charming title *The Life,
Adventures, and Unparalleled Sufferings of Andrew Oehler*. Oehler
wrote it at the ripe age of thirty, when he renounced his career as a
magician—a successful career but also one of "unparalleled sufferings," including a sojourn in a Mexican dungeon from which he was
lucky to emerge alive. He decided to labor at the trade for which he
had been raised—that of a tailor.[2]

Judging from the stir he created with his magic, Oehler was an
impressive showman and an ingenious technician. A reading of his
autobiography suggests that he deserves a place not only in the an-
nals of magic but also in the pre-history of cinema. His main illusion
was remarkably cinematic. Fortunately he gives us, in an appendix
to his book, precise details on his most spectacular achievement.

It utilized images of the magic lantern projected in a dark room
onto smoke. The swirling smoke gave the still glass-slide images a
weird, unearthly motion. This made the procedure especially suitable for such effects as "raising spirits from the dead." Oehler had
been in Paris in 1797 when the Belgian showman and scientific experimenter Étienne Gaspar Robert, called Robertson, scored resounding successes with this illusion, which he called *Fantasmagorie*.
In the disused chapel of an old convent, amid ancient tombs, Robertson called up the ghosts of leaders who had died in the French revolution. Though this created moments of official alarm, the show
remained the rage of Paris for six years and invited wide imitation.[3]
Oehler helped bring the illusion across the Atlantic. But where Robertson had accompanied his performance with a voice-over commen-
tary, Oehler added a new factor—synchronized speech. His ghosts
talked.

Oehler's autobiography reports he was born near Frankfurt-am-Main in 1781, into a family with five sons and five daughters. Andrew, the youngest of the boys, was expected to fend for himself at an early age. At ten he was apprenticed to a tailor, who treated him so cruelly that the boy decided, at thirteen, to set off into the world. He worked as a tailor's assistant in various European cities, meanwhile pursuing an obsession with magic. In every city he also studied all available scientific marvels, such as a famous tower clock in Strasbourg in which a different figure popped out at every quarter-hour, culminating in Death with his scythe. Near Lausanne, Switzerland, he worked for a tailor who occupied a fine old mansion as a tenant. When it was offered for auction, the tailor was anxious to buy it, but it was expected to fetch a sum far beyond his means. Andrew earned his undying gratitude with a bit of magic. Spreading rumors that the old building was haunted, Andrew arranged automatic contrivances in various parts of the building. Prospective buyers touring the building heard strange moans and clanking chains. The employer got the building for a pittance—a fraction of its worth. Later, in Paris, Andrew won a bonanza in a lottery. In 1797, at sixteen, he formed a partnership with a much older tailor, and they prospered. They were able to invest their profits in some Paris buildings.

The 60-year-old tailor had a 24-year-old wife, "handsome and insinuating," who wanted to visit "every place of pleasure" in the city. Her husband, not feeling up to this, was grateful to Andrew for escorting her. During months of outings they must have become familiar with Robertson's *Fantasmagorie*, just beginning its triumphant run—and with each other. Oehler's memoir tells us that he was "caught in the snare of a fatal and unlawful passion."

When the old tailor realized what was happening he swore out a warrant that landed Andrew in jail. The tailor apparently meant, by way of damages, to take over Andrew's share of their estate. But while Andrew was in jail a conflagration wiped out 150 buildings, including the partners' holdings. With the properties in ashes, the incentive was gone. Andrew was released from jail but was penniless, and his notoriety blocked further Paris employment. It led to a decision to head for America.

Years of wandering and dramatic ups and downs followed. Andrew seemed always able to pick himself up by tailoring. His tailoring led to an interest in balloons, a scientific excitement of the time that

Robertson had also taken up. Ballooning became the springboard for his magic career. Anticipating Houdini's use of spectacular public events to attract crowds to his magic performances, Andrew launched his career as a showman in 1805 in the southern United States. He was 24.

In New Orleans an assistant absconded with $2,500 and fled to Havana. Andrew shipped out in pursuit, lost the trail and embarked for Vera Cruz. He decided to resume his career in Mexico, and did so with mounting success.

In Mexico he acquired a magic lantern for his own *Fantasmagorie*. Magic lanterns had existed since the seventeenth century as a parlor entertainment for the privileged. Samuel Pepys, in an 19 August 1666 entry in his diary, mentions seeing a demonstration and buying "the lantern that shows tricks." It made "strange things to appear on a wall, very pretty." But a century later the device was still unknown to most people. In illusions like *Fantasmagorie* the lantern was operated from a masked position, unseen. The audience was unaware that any such device was involved in the effect.

In Mexico City, Oehler's balloon flights won the enthusiastic attention of government officials. The young wizard became the rage of Mexico City. The autobiography tells us he dined with the Governor and was treated "like a prince." Feted everywhere, he invited the Governor and his lady, and an elite of forty to fifty government leaders, to a performance of his most spectacular illusion.

He prepared his premises with extreme care. They included a series of adjoining rooms. The dignitaries entered through a room lined with black tapestry and hung with skeletons. The only light came from candles. The invitees proceeded into an inner room, still more sepulchral in effect. The room was dominated by an altar covered with a black cloth, topped by a skull. Beyond the altar was a brazier of burning coals. This, along with some candles, provided a mere glimmer of light.

Near the ceiling, around the entire perimeter of the room, ran a dark-colored string, invisible in the gloom. It had been rubbed with a finely ground gunpowder mixed with "spirits of wine," ready for a crucial moment in the performance.

From the altar Andrew addressed the assemblage. He announced that he was going to seek to "raise a departed spirit" and converse with it. This should not alarm anyone, he told them. There would be no danger—on command, the spirit would vanish instantly. He asked whether there was any departed soul whom anyone present especially longed to see again. Such longings were expressed. One grandee said he would dearly love to see his father again.

Now Andrew pronounced some incantations and called on the departed by name. Thunder was heard. Andrew dropped some chemicals on the burning coals, and a cloud of heavy, rolling smoke rose from the brazier. Then he stepped aside. Now came an extraordinary moment. Andrew touched a candle to the string above him. Immediately what seemed like a flash of lightning went round the perimeter of the room. At the same moment the candles went out. As a cry of alarm rose from the spectators, they suddenly saw before them, in the rising smoke, an ancient face. It began to speak. It asked—as Oehler tells it in his book—"why I had called him up from the dead, why I had disturbed his rest and repose. I answered him, and in an authoritative voice demanded of him to tell from whence he came; whether from the dismal and deep! the infernal pit! or from the happy regions of the endless felicity above! He immediately told us he came from above." The spirit's voice, Oehler tells us, was dear yet "hollow and mournful."[4]

Andrew made a request. Would the spirit, having extinguished the candles at the moment of his appearance, kindly relight them when leaving.

A moment later the ghostly image faded away The candle flames leaped up. Oehler's book explains how they had been masked rather than stifled.

The grandee said the spirit had indeed been his father. He was sure of that.

Oehler's account explains the technology of the effect. The magic lantern, masked by the altar, had sent its beam toward a slanted mirror, similarly masked, which reflected it upward toward the smoke. The smoke was close to a wall separating this room from a further room. In the further room, opposite the place where the ghost's mouth would be seen, a tube had been installed in the wall. Through this tube an assistant spoke the ghost's words. Oehler explains the synchronous effect as follows. The assistant's speech, "coming out of the end of the tube, drives the smoke a little apart, and makes an appearance like the moving of the lips of a person when he speaks."[5] It may well have been a telling effect.

The elite audience departed quietly. Andrew was not sure what the silence meant. But at four o'clock the following morning he woke to find his bedroom full of soldiers. He was taken away and incarcerated in a round pit that the autobiography describes as 150 feet deep. He was led down via steps hewed into the side of the pit. The floor was covered with straw, and furnished with a stone stool. The guard who took him down was in tears. "He advised me to make my peace with God" and explained that they would not see one another "until we met again in the eternal world." During the following months food was lowered to the prisoner by rope. It was mainly bread; fortunately, Oehler tells us, it was good bread. Still, after several months, he could hardly stand. Then, to his surprise, he was brought out, cleaned up, shaved, dressed, and taken to the Governor. He was told that a marquis visiting from Spain, perhaps familiar with Robertson's *Fantasmagorie* or one of the European imitators, had persuaded the officials that the illusion had been science, not necromancy. The Governor explained, however, that Oehler's imprisonment had been necessary to silence "the clamours of the Spanish monks and friars." They had warned that Oehler's feats "would help the Deist to argue against the true miracles of the Son of God himself."

Oehler was freed. He returned to the United States, settled in New Jersey, and resolved to remain a tailor. His memoir is so beguiling, one must recall that Oehler was a magician, practitioner of creative deception. Yet the abundance of specific detail wins confidence. His adventures remind us of how recently science and magic had been one in the public mind, with the pursuit of science regarded as a Faustian negotiation with other-worldly powers. To escape that linkage, magic performers of the nineteenth century were to make a habit of stressing that their tricks were science, and nothing supernatural.

The adventures also remind us of the magic lantern's long involvement in the prehistory of cinema. Throughout the century, the efforts of those reaching for the moving image centered on the magic lantern. Others besides Oehler mounted spectral performances, usually titled *Phantasmagoria* after Robertson's *Fantasmagorie*. They projected images either onto smoke or, by rear projection, onto layers of gauze. Between 1803 and 1810 such shows appeared in Baltimore, Boston, Providence, Salem, Savannah, and elsewhere.[6] Ghosts were the main repertoire, but the same apparatus was used to reenact large city fires reported in the news, and a New York showing offered a reenactment of a recent eruption of Mount Vesuvius. These were a kind of pre-film newsreel. Lantern slides with movable parts also existed, operated by a lever on the slide. A rocket could be shown zooming to the moon, a witch could fly across the landscape. The magic lantern became a means for elaborate storytelling. In a slide made for religious purposes Abraham, ready to sacrifice his son, held a dagger in his hand. As the projectionist operated the lever, the dagger moved menacingly toward the prostrate Isaac.[7] There were also "duplex lanterns" that allowed a projectionist to "dissolve" from one scene to another—from winter to summer, from villain to hero, from the dreamer to the dream. With such "dissolves" even the terminology of cinema was anticipated.[8] London's celebrated Poly-technic Theatre, years before the advent of film, had a projection booth that ran the width of the theater, and could bring some fifteen magic lanterns into spectacular coordinated action.[9]

But all that was marked for oblivion when the magic lantern was wed to celluloid art and gave birth to the film era.

NOTES

1. Leonard N. Beck, "Things Magical," *Quarterly Journal of the Library of Congress* (October 1974).

2. The National Union Catalogue lists surviving copies of the Oehler book in twenty-seven American libraries. Andrew Oehler, *The Life, Adventures and Unparalleled Sufferings of Andrew Oehler* (Trenton, N.J.: By the author, 1811).

3. Étienne Gaspar Robert Robertson, *Memoires Récréatifs Scientifiques et Anecdotiques*, 2 vols. (Paris: Chez l'auteur et Librarie de Wurtz, 1831). See also John Barnes, *Optical Projection*, part 2 of *Catalogue of the Collection* (St. Ives, Cornwall: Barnes Museum of Cinematography, 1970), pp. 27–28.

4. Oehler, *The Life, Adventures and Unparalleled Sufferings*, pp. 130–31.

5. *Ibid.*, appendix, pp. 221–26.

6. Charles Joseph Pecor, *The Magician on the American Stage* (Athens, Ga.: University of Georgia, 1976), pp. 106, 170.

7. *The Magic Lantern* 5 (May 1879): 5.

8. Erik Barnouw, *The Magician and the Cinema* (New York: Oxford University Press, 1961), pp. 35–38.

9. Cecil M. Hepworth, *Came the Dawn: Memories of a Film Pioneer* (London: Phoenix, 1951), pp. 15–18.

5

The Sintzenich Diaries

ARTHUR H. C. "HAL" SINTZENICH—better known in the film industry as "Snitch"—became a motion picture cameraman in 1909 and remained active for over half a century. Early in December 1912 his wife gave him a large 1913 diary, the first of sixty-one such diaries, in which he proceeded to record painstakingly periods of work, layoffs, triumphs, frustrations, earnings. He tells us precisely at what time he reported for duty each day, what time the shooting stopped, how many scenes were shot, who directed, what actors appeared—and often, who said what to whom. The diaries, which comprise a who's who of the film world during its formative years, have recently been donated to the Library of Congress by his son Cedric H. Sintzenich and are housed in the Manuscript Division.

For "Snitch"—he encouraged the use of this name, as it made things easier—the high point of his career was unquestionably his work with D. W. Griffith, whom he served as cameraman on five films during the years 1923 to 1926. Rich in informative detail, the diaries for these years will especially interest students of the silent era and of the work of Griffith. But the diaries throw light on many other chapters of film history. Sintzenich's first job was in England with Kinemacolor, the first successful color system, introduced in 1908; Snitch traveled far and wide as a Kinemacolor cameraman. He then spent eighteen months as a safari cameraman in Africa, where he managed to film a charging lion and was glad to escape with his life. In New York during World War I he became a Universal newsreel cameraman, covering the standard gamut of early newsreel assignments. He became involved in the first successful venture in underwater cinematography, which later led to work with Houdini, but he meanwhile entered the U.S. Signal Corps and was responsible for training army cameramen for World War I. After the war he worked on several films at Fort Lee studios and other studios in the New York area, photographing one of the most famous tearjerkers of the silent period, *Over the Hill to the Poor House*—said to have been

William Fox's favorite among all Fox films.[1] All this finally led to the work with Griffith and later assignments in Hollywood, India, the Soviet Union, and elsewhere.

Sintzenich was no literary stylist; his mind was technical. His observations often seem naive. It is the precision of his jottings that give the diaries their value. Production procedures are often noted. There are comments on various directors and on the work of other cameramen. Disagreements about lighting are often mentioned. There is much financial information. We gather that early cameramen were paid for days of shooting but laid off during idle intervals. Snitch, pressing for such things as a duration-of-production contract, became involved in early abortive efforts to form a cameramen's union. Film companies, including the Griffith company, were often far in arrears in salary payments. On the final pages of each year's diary Snitch notes his earnings week by week, clearly revealing his periods of economic agony.

Although the diaries are largely a record of professional activities, a fascinating human thread runs through them. Sintzenich, of German descent, was born in England, where the diaries begin. His wife, "Maimie," apparently bought him the first diary because the Kinemacolor company was about to dispatch him to the West Indies and elsewhere in the Americas for camera work and to check on Kinemacolor operations there. He was twenty-eight years old and leaving behind a young wife and two small sons. She writes in the flyleaf of the diary: "Think & love me only—Maimie xxx Dec 13th 1912." The diary entries begin the next day.

"Left home at 7 a.m. arrived office 8:10 a.m. collected apparatus. Left Waterloo 9:30 arrived alongside RSMS Orotava at Southampton 12:30. Wrote postcards to Pa, GdPa, Maimie and the boys. Sailed at 2 p.m. Dropped anchor 30 miles out on South side of I.O.W. owing to very dirty weather. Retired at 11 p.m. boat pitching slightly." (12/13/12) From then on, in diary after diary, he will record letters and postcards sent and received, and will also note—and quote—Maimie's desperate cables: "PENNILESS URGENT." These sometimes arrive when he himself is unemployed and broke. He notes money borrowed, sums cabled to Maimie, loans repaid. Reading the diaries, one cannot help wondering how such a marriage, punctuated by absences of months and years—often exceeding periods at home—can possibly hold together. Miraculously it does, to the last diary and beyond.

The Kinemacolor company, which started Snitch on his career, was organized by the celebrated Charles Urban, a dominant figure in the early British film world. Born in the United States, he had operated a kinetoscope parlor in Detroit, then went to Britain as an Edison representative. In 1898 he formed his own film company, specializing in "topicals" and dispatching "bioscope expeditions" throughout the world. In 1908 he introduced Kinemacolor, a color system patented in 1906 by G. A. Smith, who joined the Urban organization. The system was an immediate and large-scale success—but Urban soon found he had a bear by the tail.[2]

The system was sufficiently spectacular—and sufficiently simple—to invite piracy, and Urban found himself involved in endless lawsuits to protect his interests. The system also required careful technical monitoring. It involved a whirling color wheel in front of the camera and a similar wheel in front of the projector. The camera shot thirty-two frames per second onto black-and-white film. Half of these, alternative frames, were shot through a bluish-green filter; the others through a red filter. When projected through a properly synchronized color wheel, they produced impressive color images in which the colors blended in various ways through "persistence of vision." Theaters equipped to show the films became "Kinemacolor Theatres." Their showing, in brilliant color, of such events as the Delhi Durbar of 1911, celebrating the coronation of George V with imperial splendor, created a sensation around the world.

As young Snitch moved around on his travels, shooting Kinemacolor footage and regular footage, he received red-carpet treatment everywhere. In Vancouver he records: "Again went to Parliament House had audience with his Excellency the Premier Sir Richard McBride." He finds the premier delighted to be filmed "in Kinemacolor." (6/19/13) Young Snitch makes arrangements "for taking pictures from cowcatcher of CPR express going through Rockies east." He visits Kinemacolor theaters and sends reports to Mr. Urban. In some the equipment is malfunctioning; Snitch makes repairs. He keeps getting enthusiastic reports on his footage sent home. His West Indies sugar films, he is told, "have generally pleased everybody." (3/22/13) After thirteen months of travel he arrives home in a state of elation. "Bought 9 trade papers with accounts of my trip."

(1/26/14) He is at once given the task of filming the opening of Parliament by King George, and has the pleasure of seeing his film in a theater that afternoon. (2/10/14) He takes Maimie to the office to see all his American footage, and chats with Kinemacolor inventor G. A. Smith. Meanwhile he keeps trying to see his boss, Mr. Urban, about what the future may hold in the way of assignments, but Mr. Urban seems preoccupied. Then Snitch gets a shock. The Kinemacolor company has lost an important case in the Appeals Court. It plans "taking the case to the House of Lords" (4/1/14), but two weeks later, before leaving the office, Snitch is given "a notice to read . . . saying that the Natural Color Kinemacolor Co. Ltd. had gone into liquidation . . . my services would not be required after today." The company would struggle on and occasionally hire him on a per day basis, but his job was over.

He begins a whirlwind search for new employment, visiting the London Film Company, Pathé, Union Film Company, and Topical Film Company.[3] Then he hears that a Lady Grace Mackenzie needs a cameraman for a big game expedition to East Africa, goes to the Carlton Hotel, and is hired. Two days later (4/23/14) he and Lady Grace and others head for Paris and Naples, en route to Nairobi.

Here begins a long involvement with Lady Grace Mackenzie, with dramatic ups and downs and ultimately an important impact on his career. We gradually gather from the pages of the diary that "Lady Mac"—as the diary soon calls her—is backed by American investors and that the purpose of the safari is the motion picture footage he is to take, which is expected to yield a handsome profit from theater showings. Lady Mac apparently knows little about film but seems glad to leave all that to Snitch.

For a while they get on fine. In Paris he buys equipment for the expedition from Lumière, Pathé, and other companies. From Naples they set sail on the S. S. *Gascon* for Mombasa, from where they will go by train to Nairobi, continuing from there with "fifty boys and safari outfit. . . ." (6/1/14)

Throughout this period the diaries are full of references to Lady Mac. "Lady Mac made many purchases from hawkers." (4/30/14) "Repaired Lady Mac's Kodak." (5/13/14) "Shopping etc. in morning for Lady Mac." (5/21/14) "Up early & out with Lady Mac & Mr. Shelley, buying and making final arrangements." (6/1/14) "Slept in

Lady Mac's tent last night." (6/3/14) There is no further explanation of the last entry.

The expedition includes a doctor with a somewhat Dickensian name—Dr. Dudgeon. He is soon very busy as practically everyone falls ill. Snitch has constant fevers and agonizing abdominal pains, but the work grinds on. One night, "was up with Syd Lydford nearly all the time expecting a visit to our cave as we had elephant, rhino & lions all around us, who occasionally got our wind & set up an awful noise. . . . Lizards, bats & small snakes run & fly about in the cave & keep us company at night." (10/31/14) Occasionally useful footage is obtained, including what Snitch later describes as "the first authentic motion picture of a charging lion." In December they are back in Nairobi, developing and editing.

But the strain has had its effect. There are arguments with Lady Mac—"showeries," he calls them. A New Year's Eve entry, written in Nairobi, tells us: "Not feeling at all happy today, cannot forget a few things said to me by Lady Mac last night. Joined party for New Year celebrations for appearances only." (12/31/14) Two weeks later: "Was cleaning & making up negatives in Lady Mac's room when we had a misunderstanding & led to words. I was not feeling at all well & in pain, lost my temper & grossly insulted her for which I feel an awful cad & dare not hope to be forgiven." (1/15/15) Next day he apologizes, but a few days later Lady Mac decides to send him back to England. He sails from Mombasa around the Cape of Good Hope. The ship shifts course to avoid mine fields. World War I has begun; for the principal belligerents, areas of Africa are stakes in the struggle.

Arriving home, he immediately has an appendix operation. On the same day he notes that "Kinemacolor lost their appeal in the House of Lords today." Meanwhile we gather that Lady Mac, who has gone back to New York with all the film, still owes him a substantial sum in unpaid salary. He writes and cables reminders, saying he is "absolutely broke," but without results. After six weeks of these efforts he notes in the diary: "I have had no reply to my letter nor my last four cables sent to Lady Mackenzie in New York." Snitch's innumerable relatives (his father had fourteen children by three marriages) are furious and say he should go to New York to confront her and her backers, and his brother Archie offers him a loan for this purpose. Snitch books passage on the SS *Adriatic*, sailing from Liverpool. As he leaves, Maimie writes in his diary: "May God bless & bring you safely Home to your darling wee boys and ever faithful and loving wife Maimie." (5/12/15) Two weeks later he has the first of several confrontations with Lady Mac. "Had a showery with Lady Mac re my affairs & ended with hot words & she accused me of coming to New York for the purpose of blackmailing her. I told her I wished a prompt settlement of her obligations to me." (5/28/15) He also sees one of her backers, a Mr. Joyce. "He told me . . . he had loaned Lady M a small fortune & refused to put up any more money as he saw no possible chance of getting it back, through her mismanagement." (6/22/15) He also sees a lawyer and decides to bring suit if no settlement is reached. As this will take money, the Lady Mac pursuit is interspersed with job hunting. He sees a Mr. Wood at Essanay; calls on Universal, Éclair, Fox. "Took a streetcar to 130th Street crossed on the Ferry and took another car to Fort Lee, where I walked up to the Solax factory," (6/10/15)[4] He finds an old film acquaintance from England but no work. Another day: "called on Harold Ives & Co . . . later called on Gaumont's then down to Fulton Street to see Mr. Hemmerts. Ret'd home feeling dead beat & very tired." (6/14/15)

A fortunate circumstance comes to his aid. On June 7 *Lady Mackenzie's Big Game in Motion Pictures* opens at the Lyceum Theatre on 45th Street near Times Square and is praised by several papers, with Snitch's lion charge called "the sensation" of the film. He starts taking people "to see my pictures." (6/9/15) Unfortunately newspaper attention goes entirely to Lady Mackenzie; neither the film nor any newspaper mentions Sintzenich, and she herself plays down the cameraman's role. He was in no danger, she tells an interviewer. "The cameraman has always two armed boys to guard him." She also says the film involved "four operators," which causes Snitch to write indignant letters to the press, (6/16/15) apparently to no avail.

Nevertheless he finds work. A Mr. Whipple, chief of Universal's newsreel Animated Weekly, offers him a job as cameraman.[5] He accepts and goes into a whirlwind of "topical" assignments: a baby parade on Staten Island; a boat race at Poughkeepsie; an undertakers' convention with a display of opulent new caskets. He is sent to City Island to film "ladies bathing suits in the European style, one piece costumes, tight-fitting to the figure without skirts, which they are trying to introduce into this country." (7/9/15) A few days later he records that censors have banned his film. He also films Harry K.

Thaw on his acquittal for the murder of Stanford White; Bernarr Macfadden doing physical culture exercises; and, on the same day, "President Wilson arriving in New York with his fiancee." (10/8/15) Later he covers a lunch of the American Defense Society, where "I had a very pleasant chat with Col. Roosevelt about Africa. . . ."(1/5/ 16)

Meanwhile Universal suddenly asks him to help with studio production, and he is involved in an avalanche of fiction films. We get a glimpse of the speed with which short features are thrown together. In mid-September he begins work on *Blood Heritage*, directed by a Mr. Shaw, starring a Miss Gray. In mid-October he begins another film for Mr. Shaw in a new studio at Fort Lee, again with Miss Gray. On November 1 he begins a third film, *A Social Butterfly*, and records doing thirty scenes in a day. This work is interspersed with newsreel assignments, and an offer from representatives of Henry Ford to serve as cameraman on the Peace Ship about to sail for Europe—an offer canceled by Ford when he learns that Sintzenich is a British citizen. (11/2/15)

His notes on *Angel in the Attic*, starring Florence Lawrence, provide a revealing insight into studio production: "Everything ready for an early start with Miss Lawrence in a picture titled *The Angel in the Attic*. The set was up & I had apparatus all ready, but Miss L. on arriving about 11 a.m. on reading the story refused to play the part, so nothing was done." (2/26/16) Two days later he notes that Mr. Kelley, the director assigned to the film, "did not put in an appearance today as he was home writing a script for Miss Lawrence." (2/ 28/16) Two days later they are in production with the new script, although Florence Lawrence again proves "very difficult to handle." (3/1/16)[6]

During these months Snitch works long hours daily, including Sundays. It has enabled him to cable money to Maimie in answer to her desperate pleas, but he is approaching exhaustion. On March 11, again summoned for Sunday work, he objects and is at once fired by Universal. He dares not tell Maimie. Mr. Kelley, his most recent director, sends him $100 to tide him over. As with previous disasters, the crisis brings an important new opportunity.

John Ernest Williamson, a Scots immigrant descended from a line of seafaring Scotsmen, wants to reveal the wonders of the deep via underwater cinematography. In Nassau, Bahamas, he has constructed a "Williamson submarine"—actually, a windowed chamber reached through a long pipe projecting downward from a surface vessel. Photographic tests have been made from the chamber by his associate Carl L. Gregory. Encouraged by their success, Williamson decides to exploit the device via a fiction film, comes to New York for a cinematographer, and hires Sintzenich. A diary entry (4/11/16) records that Snitch is to leave for Nassau within three days. By the end of the month he is making descents into the underwater chamber and filming a "panorama of the ocean bottom" through its circular window, four feet in diameter. On shore he constructs a dark room and develops the tests. Within days they are shooting their feature, which involves underwater struggles over a treasure chest. "Scenes of Gardner & Barringer under water . . . B finds it and G comes over and they fight for it, G cutting what he thought to be B's air pipe, which was his own & falls over dead." Later Snitch gets "shark pictures—which turned out A-1." He prepares the underwater footage for tinting, sails for New York, returns to Nassau for additional footage, cables money to Maimie—who is "penniless"—and under great pressure starts editing the film, now entitled *The Submarine Eye*. He finally returns to New York on the *Morro Castle*, gets an offer from Vitagraph to go to Alaska, but turns it down. Euphoria surrounds the submarine project. He writes reassuringly to Maimie, "enclosing the comic section of the Sunday *American* for the children." (3/10/17) He begins running the film—nine reels long—for prospective buyers; works on titles for a Spanish version; runs the film "for the musicians." (4/2/17) On May 27 *The Submarine Eye* opens in New York at the Liberty Theatre and scores a triumph. The theater is packed for weeks, according to *The Moving Picture World.* The underwater shots win loud plaudits, and "the suspense is all that could be asked."[7]

Williamson and his brother are "independents" with no distribution setup, which means that success depends on selling "state rights" and other regional rights to various distributors. The New York premiere apparently brings a rush of such sales, and Snitch is kept busy preparing and sending out prints—to Minneapolis, Atlanta, Philadelphia, Pittsburgh; then to London, South Africa, and elsewhere.

Snitch's 1917 diary shows that he is usually getting only forty dollars a week when working, but he is surrounded by signs of rising fortune. In the midst of work on *The Submarine Eye* his lawsuit against Lady Grace Mackenzie comes up in City Court and is unopposed; Snitch gets a judgment for "$1909 & costs." (5/10/17) He still has the problem of collecting, but we learn that Lady Mac has married a Mr. Frisbee, a Buffalo businessman who seems determined to end the feud. Frisbee offers Snitch $300 in cash, which Snitch accepts. (5/16/17) The settlement brings a complete change of atmosphere. Snitch gets a call from Lady Mac and has tea with the newlyweds at the Astor. Mr. Frisbee engages Snitch for further editing of the African footage, to create a new feature film. They are all suddenly very friendly. Snitch accompanies Mr. Frisbee to Gimbels to look for a suit for Mr. Frisbee, but they do not find what he wants. Meanwhile the magician Harry Houdini gets in touch with Snitch and hires him to film various Houdini appearances, including underwater escape acts performed at Westport, Connecticut, and Atlantic City, New Jersey, and a straitjacket escape performed while hanging upside down over a Times Square crowd. For months Snitch and Williamson are in constant touch with Houdini.[8] Beginning to feel secure and even flush, Snitch makes some purchases of his own: "Purchased a silk hat and straw hat." (6/14/17) "Purchased waistcoats, also to Whitehouse and Hardy for some shoes." (6/15/17) *Scientific American* interviews him about underwater cinematography.

In the midst of this rising good fortune, Snitch receives one of the most severe jolts of his career. He gets a series of letters from Archie, the brother who loaned him money to pursue Lady Mac to New York. Archie has been accused of making the loan to help Snitch escape military service in Britain and has been told that he himself will have to do military service unless Snitch returns to perform his duty. (3/17/17) Archie, like Snitch, has dependents and is appealing the case. Snitch reassures Archie that he will not leave him in the lurch, but both wait with apprehension. In November Archie reports a new turn. The authorities now feel that if Snitch enlists in the United States—by now allied with Britain in the war—the case against Archie may be dropped.[9] Archie cables: "WILL CARRY WEIGHT IN APPEAL IF OFFICIALLY CABLED JOINED UP." (11/24/17) Snitch acts swiftly. Within days he is in Washington visiting the Signal Corps; early in December, at the urging of Signal Corps personnel, he takes out first papers at the U.S. Supreme Court. On the day after Christmas he enters the Signal Corps as master signal

electrician. Within days he is back in New York with official orders
to organize a School of Military Cinematography at Columbia University. The university offers space in the basement of Philosophy
Hall for a "Cine Lab" (1/11/18) but Snitch rejects it because of
steam pipes.[10] He eventually gets space in Havemeyer Hall. Space for
barracks is earmarked on the grounds of the Cathedral of St. John
the Divine. By the end of January Snitch has outlined a curriculum,
made estimates for equipment purchases, interviewed candidates for
the school, and begun lectures on photography. (1/24/18) A "new
reflex camera . . . entirely new novel & advanced departure," rouses
his excitement. (1/25/18) Victor Fleming, known to Snitch as cameraman for Douglas Fairbanks[11] and "an awfully good fellow," joins the
teaching staff and becomes head of the unit. (2/16/18) Soon both
achieve the rank of second lieutenant. Between lectures and work-
shops the men drill and do semaphore practice on the football field
at 116th Street. They meet "ladies from Barnard College."

We learn that Maimie is having "a rotten time . . . through money
troubles." (5/3/18) Snitch manages to cable her seventy-five dollars.
He himself falls ill and is rushed to a hospital—"coughed my heart
out"—but is soon back in action. He selects eight men for immediate overseas duty.

In May a new development changes Snitch's life. "Capt. Sears
called me in his office, told me Congress had passed a bill whereby
all friendly aliens in the Army can become citizens immediately."
(5/18/18) Six men in the film unit—Bove, Dadetto, Lipsgar, Mill-
stine, Murray, and Sintzenich—are taken to City Hall and come back
American citizens. In June the men are all taken to the Lyric Theatre
to see the official U.S. war film *Pershing's Crusaders*—which Snitch
finds "very rotten." (6/11/18) Meanwhile the war is moving to a climax and in August Snitch and others board the SS *Leviathan* (formerly the German *Vaterland*) at Hoboken and are off for Europe
with 1,300 troops and a crew of 2,000. They land in France.

It is not clear what expectations Snitch has had for overseas activity. If he expected combat photography, he is soon disillusioned. He
spends weeks making "identification photos" of soldiers and "desk
photos" of officers. Then, to his surprise, he is suddenly ordered to
London, apparently for similar duty. He docks in Southampton and
phones Maimie; getting no answer, he boards a train for London.
"Arrived home at 8:30 to a very surprised little family who had no

idea I was in England." (9/30/18) A few days later he is again making "desk portraits" of officers and also documenting activities at U.S. camps, airfields, and hospitals in Britain. He also renews contact with Charles Urban and other Kinemacolor alumni. Then suddenly the war is over. London goes wild. Ten days later Snitch learns that he will be able to take Maimie and the children back to the United States.

But first there are more official duties. He is ordered to Dover to cover President Wilson's arrival for the peace conferences. He and Victor Fleming accompany the presidential train to London and shoot the arrival in Downing Street. Snitch is also ordered to prepare photographic equipment for a unit bound for Archangel to counter the Bolshevik revolution. He shoots more desk portraits, medal-pinning ceremonies, camps, and airfields and is promoted to first lieutenant.

When he comes down with the flu, "Maimie delights in rubbing me back & front with embrocation & dope & insists on dabbing me with cotton wool. Feel like a stuffed owl." In June the family finally boards the SS *Plattsburgh* at Liverpool. Maimie and the boys have a cabin but Snitch must bunk with the officers. "We were very disappointed . . . but it is a Navy rule." There are "beaucoup babies and beaucoup squalls." (6/4/19)

The Sintzenichs arrive in New York almost penniless. The next day Snitch is paid off and discharged, and they pay fifty dollars as the first month's rent on an apartment at 189 Claremont Avenue—near Snitch's old haunts at Columbia University and also a short walk to the Fort Lee ferry. Lady Mac promptly invites them all to dinner, and they have a "very happy evening" with the Frisbees. Meanwhile Snitch is scurrying around film offices, trying to pick up where he left off. He learns that Williamson is in Nassau. He accepts a short assignment in Chicago, and while there gets a wire that Williamson wants him in Nassau. Snitch wires Williamson that he is available "for the duration of the picture at $125 per week." Williamson agrees to the terms.

At the time Snitch entered the Signal Corps, he had reason to believe he was moving toward the top of his profession. But to resume the rise was not easy. A cloud hung over the effort. Hollywood is seldom mentioned in the Sintzenich diaries of 1919 to 1922, although the westward tide was the root of his problems. It is as though he was reluctant to face the fact that he might now be in the wrong place.

On the other hand, he had reasons for staying. He had had success here, and enough activity remained to provide constant hope. And the Sintzenichs soon had other attachments to the area. They moved to Tenafly and then Englewood, both convenient to Fort Lee. Snitch took up gardening. They were a family again and anxious to feel settled.

The new Williamson project—centering on sharks and using East-man's Panchromatic film (Sintzenich's first mention of this product, not yet in commercial distribution but available experimentally)—lasts six weeks, and he is back in New York calling on Metro, Fox, Famous Players, Selznick, and Solax. The next three years are a kaleidoscope of jobs, mostly of short duration, involving a cataract of names, known and unknown, and films, most of which are long forgotten. An unnamed film starring Elsie Janis—"a very difficult subject to light"—with location work in Tarrytown; "took scenes of Miss Janis driving a car at 60 m.p.h. round the fountain in a circle." (9/25/19) For Selznick, *Out of the Night* starring Olive Thomas, who is mentioned in a later diary as having died in Paris of "mercurial poisoning." Snitch is first camera, but a few days later he is second camera to Henry Cronjager, shooting *Greater than Fame* with Elaine Hammerstein, directed by Alan Crosland.[12] (11/4/19) The following month he is first camera again in the Selznick film *The Woman God Sent*, with Zeena Keefe, filmed at the Biograph studio and directed by Larry Trimble, whom Snitch finds "quite a comedian." He shoots an unnamed biblical film in Fort Lee (1/31/20), and Fox hires him for a location stint at a New Jersey iron mine, sometimes working 400 feet down in ankle-deep water, for a film starring Margaret Clayton. "At the mine we took scenes of Miss Clayton on horseback catching the rope ladder dropped from a blimp & climbing up. . . . Photographed 51 scenes." (3/28/20) Snitch also works on an episode of the serial *Fantomas*, and films Pearl White in *A Virgin Romance* when her regular cameraman is off for Yom Kippur. (9/21/20)

Most of these assignments are brief. They involve unlimited hours and intermittent pay. Two or more cameramen are often "cranking" side by side, but sometimes they work simultaneously on different scenes. A cameraman may supervise laboratory work, or edit, or even act; in one film Snitch is handed a robe and becomes a judge. His earnings sometimes rise to $175 a week but often fall much lower. The period might have been a disaster except for one major success, the Fox film *Over the Hill to the Poor House*.[13]

Work on this began in April 1920 under the direction of Harry Millarde and occupied Snitch on a daily basis until the premiere on September 17. The star of the film was Mrs. Mary Carr.[14] Throughout this time, the diary reflects rising enthusiasm. We get glimpses of the elusive William Fox. "At the studio by 9:15 & was ready to crank at 9:30. Took scenes with Mrs. Carr and Mr. Sullivan. Mr. Fox came up and kidded Mr. Millarde about the musicians (two), cello and violin. He asked whether it was the actors or cameraman who needed the music." (5/17/20) Snitch learns from Mr. Millarde that Fox is "very happy with my photography."

In various diary entries, Sintzenich mentions working on "double exposures" or "visions." "In the studio making double exposures with Mrs. Carr and her two daughters." (5/19/20)

One day, at the end of a day of shooting, Mrs. Carr offers Sintzenich a ride in her taxi, since she lives close to the Fort Lee ferry. Later she and five of her six children visit the Sintzenichs in Englewood. Snitch sometimes refers to her as "Mother Carr." He now has a "standing invitation" for the uptown rides. Snitch mentions bringing in baskets of lettuce and cherries for Mrs. Carr. They sometimes eat their lunch together at the studio. The friendship leads to a curious encounter. Mr. Carr—previously unmentioned—visits the studio and in a "very abrupt manner" requests that Snitch no longer have lunch with Mrs. Carr "or be in her company at any time." Snitch comments: "Poor old soul has evidently a screw loose." (7/16/20)

There are repeated references to William Fox's growing enthusiasm. In July he presses Millarde to finish the film "this week." On August 10 they work all night—till 5:30 A.M. Snitch gets home at 7:30 A.M. Then he learns that Fox has "taken the picture away from Mr. Millarde" and is making final touches himself. Snitch is kept busy in September making "inserts." Fox has him "double-expose" the title *Over the Hill to the Poor House* over an old shawl. (9/16/20) The film opens the following day at the Astor Theatre.

There is "not one dry eye in the house." There are fine reviews. For weeks the Astor displays a "House Sold Out" sign. (10/31/20) Sintzenich has a "photographed by" credit and gets numerous congratulations. He gets an offer from another company but declines it, feeling he is "well fixed with the Fox Co." He has reason to think so, but the film is so successful that Fox decides to move his operations to the West Coast. After *Over the Hill to the Poor House*, Hollywood becomes the center of Fox production. In the end Sintzenich's moment of glory contributes to his economic dilemma.

References to flagging New York activity have already peppered the diary, "Things in general seem very slack." (3/18/20) As he renews the job hunt he notes: "Another day of waiting and watching. . . . There is absolutely nothing doing anywhere." (2/8/20) There are rumors of activity in the offing, but most peter out.

Throughout these months the remaining cameramen increasingly band together. Snitch has mentioned joining a Society of Motion Picture Craftsmen, to which he has paid a twenty-five-dollar initiation fee, (9/15/19) but a few months later he becomes a member of the United Society of Cinematographers. (5/5/20) He describes a meeting at which they learn of demands being made by laboratory workers for a 50 percent wage increase, (6/7/20) and another meeting at which a spokesman for the International Alliance of Theatrical Stage Employees talks on "unionism." (11/1/20) Soon afterwards Snitch joins a new organization, the Motion Picture Photographers Association, paying sixty-five dollars to cover initiation and three months' dues. This group becomes the focus of his activity. He designs a union emblem with the slogan "honesty, integrity, ability." (11/27/20) The diary indicates that Snitch is moving into a leadership position. He rents quarters for the group. (2/4/21) An attorney helps them frame contract objectives. (3/16/21) They also hold craft meetings, at one of which Edward J. Steichen talks to them on "What's the Matter with the Movies." (4/2/21)

The group is small—apparently some twenty-four members. Snitch mentions sending out twenty-four special delivery letters to summon members to a meeting, at which fifteen members appear. There is no indication of what takes place but Snitch gets home at 1:30 A.M.

The group is referred to as a "union" but also as "the club." "Was at the club & all the members who are at liberty turned up during the day." It is a base for job hunting, exchange of information, and messages. One gathers that the show of militancy heartens the group, but that there is little they can do for themselves in a shrinking market. And while they share problems, they are also competitors for the same dwindling jobs. At one point Snitch confides to his diary: "I have grave doubts as to the honour and integrity of one of our members. . . ." (3/16/21)

In the determination to hang on, a factor must have been David Wark Griffith—at least, for many in the group. While whole studios moved west, he had done the reverse. Proclaiming his disenchantment with Hollywood, he had established his own studio at Mamaroneck. His presence had immense symbolic significance for the New York film colony, giving hope to Snitch and others.

The diaries had already mentioned various attempts to contact the Griffith studio. Early in 1921—on the heels of *Over the Hill to the Poor House*—Snitch has visited a Wynne Jones at the Griffith office and been " 'graciously" received. A few months later: "Met Mr. Billy Bitzer for the first time today and had quite a talk with him." (5/3/21)[15] A Mr. Lloyd, also of the Griffith office, promises him a tryout if they need an "extra camera." (5/6/21) During the following months these contacts seem to be leading to action. Lloyd asks him "to call around about May 5." (4/27/22) Lloyd then introduces him to Henrik Sartov, who has become Griffith's leading cameraman. Visiting the Griffith studio, Snitch has a three-hour talk with Sartov and is introduced to Griffith himself. (6/1/22) But later he learns that nothing has been settled; in fact, "the project" has been postponed.

All this is interspersed with further spasmodic jobs—most of them unrewarding. The Lady Mackenzie saga makes a reappearance, by no means the last. Work on the African footage has yielded a new feature film titled *Heart of Africa*, in which Sintzenich is credited with the photography. Mr. Frisbee says it will premiere in Buffalo early in May. The Frisbees now want him to shoot a follow-up film on St. Andros Island, near Nassau, about the life and habits of flamingos. Snitch agrees, and in August he sets up camp on the island, builds a blind, and in all-night vigils gradually moves it closer. He is "bitten by millions of mosquitoes" and returns with "a dozen huge boils on left leg." He feels very sick and is increasingly worried about his health. Diary entries have mentioned painful piles and a suspicion of stomach ulcers. His 1922 earnings are only $2,559.

Inserted into the diary at November 5, 1922, is a strange memento—a crayon-decorated card from one of the Sintzenich boys. "From Bubbles. Daddy will get work. God will give Him it."

Late in December he hears that Sartov has "picked me to go South with the Griffith Co." But Christmas passes without further word. Then, on January 3, the summons comes.

The diaries covering Sintzenich's work with Griffith, 1923 to 1926, will be studied minutely by Griffith scholars. They involve five silent features: *The White Rose* (1923), *America* (1924), *Isn't Life Wonderful?* (1924), *Sally of the Sawdust* (1925), and *That Royle Girl* (1926). They contain fascinating glimpses of the master at work. There is room here to mention only a few aspects of Griffith that are illuminated by the diaries.

They constantly reflect the wide awe that Griffith still commands throughout these years. He is always "Mr. Griffith" or "the Governor." On train trips he may play poker with actors and cameramen but an "invisible barrier" surrounds him. President and Mrs. Harding come to visit him on location. Reporters besiege him. And he speaks on the radio with an eloquence and resonance that prompt Maimie to say: "A man who can talk like that—no wonder he can make films."

On the other hand, the diaries offer evidence of Griffith's mounting financial problems, his gradual loss of artistic independence, and finally the slippage in his industry status.

At the start of 1923 there is no hint of the decline. And Snitch's entry into the inner circle has the quality of initiation ritual.

The January 3 summons to Mamaroneck, which reaches him in town, tells him to bring his camera. "Went home got the apparatus & took the 2:28 from 125th St. Arrived at the studio in a snowstorm. Loaded up & took my first shot, close up, of Miss Marsh.[16] Continued working until 8 o'clock. Caught the B&W [Boston & Westchester] 8:40 train from Larchmont & got home at 10 o'clock. Everybody feeling much happier tonight with the bright prospects in view for me." However, not a word has been said to him all day about his status. He has no idea whether he has actually become a Griffith cameraman; and if so, at what salary. (1/3/23)

Next day the same ritual is repeated. Long hours of shooting with "Miss Marsh & Mr. Novello."[17] Then they all sit down and look at scenes from *Way Down East*, *Intolerance*, and *Orphans of the Storm*, and discuss lighting problems. No word to Snitch about his status. Next day, the same story. They shoot from early morning till 8 P.M. Snitch writes in his diary: "Things in general going along about the same, but nothing definite has been arranged with me, as to whether I am satisfactory etc. & no mention as to its terms etc." (1/5/23) Next day he again shoots from morning until 8 P.M., then has dinner with Sartov and others, after which they all go to the projection room and look at five reels of the new footage—"I am happy to say mine was as good as the rest"—after which Mr. Griffith has a print of *Little Lord Fauntleroy*, with Mary Pickford, run off for further discussions about lighting. Snitch finally catches an 11:30 P.M. train and gets home long after midnight. He still has no word of clarification. (1/7/23)

All this goes on for four more days, including a twelve-hour Sunday stint during which Griffith "is in a cheerful mood . . . singing most of the time between shots," and Sartov does some beautiful lighting . . . of which I made notes." (1/7/23) Finally, on January 12—his tenth day of work—Snitch is informed that he is hired— "which is the best news I have had in years." (1/12/23) His salary, $175 per week, is less than he had hoped for and expected; but when told he will be paid between films, as a regular member of the company, he is delighted.

The following day is Sunday, and a day off. "The *Telegraph* had an item *re* myself being with DWG which was written in by Maimie & headed 'The Faithful Wife.' " (1/14/23) On Monday Snitch buys a suit.

The film on which they have been working, *The White Rose*, is to have four cameramen for the location work in the New Orleans area: Henrik Sartov, Billy Bitzer, Hal Sintzenich, and Frank Diem. The situation seems to keep them all on edge, basking in the master's occasional praise. Griffith apparently tries to dole this out evenhandedly, but in a way that must unnerve others. During work at New Iberia, Snitch writes with apparent pleasure: "They had been working already four days on the location when Mr. Griffith asked me if I could [do] any better setup than the one they were using. Took a tour around & set up in the opposite direction & when Mr. Griffith saw it he called Mr. Bitzer & Mr. Sartov & told them that I had found a far better way than any they had used." (2/14/23)[18]

Bits of praise sometimes come indirectly via Carol Dempster. During work on *America* Snitch notes: "Miss Dempster told me she saw a lot of the film run off last night & said I had a number of beautiful shots, complimenting me on them." She tells him DWG was pleased with them.[19]

The rivalry between cameramen sometimes involved lighting. Snitch at first admired Sartov but eventually got exasperated with Sartov's "backlighting everything." He also objected to Sartov's determination to mix sunlight with artificial light. *Isn't Life Wonderful?*, a film about Germany during its runaway inflation, was shot partly on location there. A scene of "Hans & Inga drawing the cart & being stopped & questioned by a gang of hungry ruffians" was shot on a sunny day in woods near Potsdam. Sartov called for "lights to travel with the camera. I could not stand that hokum any longer so let out." Snitch considered reflectors not only adequate but preferable. He apparently lost the debate. "Worked all day in beautiful weather, but I by no means liked the camera shots picked by the Governor. . . ." A week later the diary entries are still agitating the matter. "Some day somebody is going to wake up and maybe it will be me." (8/18/24)

Snitch is condescending toward Billy Bitzer in matters of lighting. During work on a Lionel Barrymore scene for *America*, "Billy fooled about with the lights not knowing what he was doing half the time & it was after 1 o'clock as usual before we started shooting." (12/19/23) Several passages suggest an edginess toward Bitzer. "Tried to get the $15 Billy owed me but as expected was out of luck." (3/1/24) Later Bitzer tries to sell him a "number board." (11/4/ 25)

A Griffith habit illuminated by the diaries is the continuation of shooting long after initial showings. *The White Rose* was shown in New London, Connecticut, and Montclair, New Jersey, in mid-May 1923, after which there was much reshooting and a complete revision of the ending. The New York premiere was on May 22 at the Lyric Theatre but two days later Snitch was shooting retakes of Ivor Novello including "one at the cigar counter & one in Ball Room." (5/24/23) On some of the later pictures this process went on for weeks.

On February 10, 1924, Snitch mentions a showing of *America* in South Norwalk, Connecticut. On the same day he is shooting scenes for its Valley Forge sequence in nearby Westchester, impelled by the arrival of ideal blizzard weather for "the men in bare feet in the snow trying to pull the big wagon." (2/10/24) The Battle of Princeton is shot the following day, in time to be included four days later in a showing in Danbury, Connecticut, when Snitch is shooting Washington's inauguration. Two days later they are remaking "the stockade scenes." On the day of the New York premiere, February 21, Snitch is still doing close-ups of Carol Dempster, and during the following week does retakes of "Miss Dempster & Hamilton" and new "stockade scenes with 30 extras."

The diary passages dealing with *America* provide glimpses of Griffith as an organizer of massive action. Most of the film was shot in Westchester County, although "inserts" were later taken at landmarks in Boston, Washington, and elsewhere. Major photography began on August 23, 1923, and continued at a backbreaking pace. Snitch apparently shuttled between second-unit comedy sequences directed by a Mr. Noble and spectacle shots directed by Griffith himself. "Over at the studio by 9:30. Worked in the studio with Mr. Noble until noon when Mr. Griffith sent for me on location. Worked with him all afternoon taking Paul Revere's ride." They try to get the horse to jump over a creek but fail. The day's entry concludes: "Understand Mr. Noble had a poor time with his colored people & the water stuff, the women refusing to go under in the baptismal scenes." (9/2/23)

Much battle action was filmed in the wooded hills around Brewster and Somers, Westchester County, New York, where hundreds of extras were assembled. "Most of the extras are housed in barns & tents, about 30 cots to a tent, and the mess tent accommodating one half while the hotel dining room the other. The whole Co. is run like a military camp." A National Guard unit and state police help out. A bugle blows "reveille" at 6 A.M. and "mess" at 6:45 A.M. Location work is scheduled for 7:30 A.M. (9/20/23)

During an "attack on the stockade by Indians British & soldiers & the burning of the buildings," thirteen cameramen grind simultaneously. (9/24/23) We gather that Pathé newsreel cameramen sometimes join them to cover large actions. A battle sequence involving 500 extras takes a whole day to prepare. "We eventually took the battle scene about 5 o'clock & had to retake it as the Colonials used the wrong flag." (9/25/23) On a later day a gunner's hand is blown off by a premature explosion. (10/2/23)

One day Griffith summons Snitch to help plan camera deployment for a battle sequence. Griffith is mounted, while Snitch trots along on foot; in this fashion they cover several miles. Snitch's reaction to the episode is satisfaction that he was able to keep up with Griffith. (9/21/23)

Snitch and others have bouts with flu but the work continues at a grueling pace, seven days a week, often until midnight. Occasionally Snitch misses his last train and sleeps in a studio dressing room. A few times Griffith sends him home in his limousine.

A Sunday entry: "Worked hard until after midnight when the crowd went home but Mr. G. asked me to stay & work in the 'White House' in case Sartov caved in, as he was sick." Snitch gets home at 2 A.M. (2/17/24) The following day they do Valley Forge close-ups, scenes at Washington's headquarters, and other shots. "I took the last close-up with Miss Dempster at 1 A.M. Mr. Stitch made inserts with Billy Bitzer and Joe. When we finished the Governor told us we could 'go to the movies' but not to stay out late." (2/18/24)

The New York premiere is three days later; Maimie buys a new gown for the occasion. The diary summarizes reactions: "The first half was tremendously received, but the crowd was evidently disappointed with the second." (2/21/24) A few critics considered it a Griffith masterpiece, particularly in its battle sequences. But there was criticism of the long explanatory subtitles. And there was no stampede to the box office.

The most poignant aspects of the diaries on the Griffith years are the gradual unfolding of his financial situation and the erosion of his standing in the industry. We see him still getting worshipful attention, but the ground is clearly crumbling under his feet.

After completion of *The White Rose*, Sintzenich is surprised to receive notice that he will be laid off until the next film. He points out to Griffith that he was promised payment between pictures, and that his salary—$175 a week—was predicated on this. Griffith seems troubled, says he does not wish to lose Sintzenich, and that "I would be kept on salary between pictures." (6/2/23) On the strength of this assurance, the Sintzenichs move from Englewood to an apartment in Pelham, not far from the Griffith studio.

But Griffith, deeply in debt and carrying a huge studio overhead, needs a success on the scale of *The Birth of a Nation*—or at least of *Way Down East*—to stay afloat, and his staff becomes painfully aware of this. Toward the end of the work on *America* they are asked to hold their checks "until after the end of the picture, so as to help Mr. Griffith with his terrific expenses." (12/19/23) At the time of the premiere, the studio is also four weeks in arrears in the issuing of salary checks. The mixed reaction at the premiere becomes doubly ominous. A week later Snitch is asked to come to the office, and is told they are "shutting down & would have to dispense with my services until the next picture." Snitch is not surprised. The diary even expresses appreciation for "the manner in which it was done." (2/29/24)

Three months later he hears that Griffith has chosen him to go to Germany on a new film, eventually titled *Isn't Life Wonderful?* A deal with Adolf Zukor of Paramount—it has been described as "an undercover deal"[20]—apparently made this project possible. But Griffith has mortgaged his future to Paramount to stave off disaster. Snitch is told he will get $175 a week while in Germany, but $200 thereafter. (6/30/24) As the company sails for Germany aboard the SS *George Washington*, Griffith seems in a good mood again, but on the return trip he is seldom seen, and the group is troubled. In Mamaroneck the work on *Isn't Life Wonderful?* is resumed, in sets built to match the German locations.

A diary entry records: "Received my cheque today but not the promised increase." (9/30/24) Snitch raises the question at the company office but gets evasive answers. As the shooting of *Isn't Life Wonderful?* is completed, Snitch again goes off the payroll, but is promised he will *positively* be on the next picture. (12/8/24)

But the final checks for *Isn't Life Wonderful?* are only partial payments, accompanied by promissory notes. Sintzenich has problems at the bank with Griffith's notes. At the bank a Mr. Hendriks tells him he wants "to investigate DW & asked me to fill out a form." (1/29/25)

But Griffith is again able to launch a new film—*Sally of the Sawdust*, with Carol Dempster, W. C. Fields, Alfred Lunt, and others—to be made for Paramount. Griffith's Mamaroneck studio is sold; the new film will be shot at the Paramount studios, with Griffith as a Paramount staff employee. When Snitch inquires about his own status, with a reminder that Griffith promised he would be on the film, Snitch is told: "Mr. Griffith has no right to make promises." (2/18/25)

Nevertheless Snitch gets an offer from Paramount—$150 a week. He is furious but accepts; he continues with Griffith both on *Sally of the Sawdust* and *That Royle Girl*—a story Griffith has tried to reject. (7/16/25) But the old aura is gone. Snitch quotes one of the Sintzenich boys, after a family visit to the studio: "Mr. Griffith is awfully quiet, he is always thinking of something else." (11/9/24)

With the completion of *That Royle Girl*—again with Carol Dempster and W. C. Fields—Snitch asks Griffith what he thinks will be next. "DW said he did not know whether there would be any next." (1/6/26)

Two weeks later Snitch writes in his diary: "Things are certainly dead & from all accounts, with several companies packing up and going to California, it looks bad for New York." (1/20/26) A few months later Snitch himself is heading west.

POSTSCRIPTS

Snitch has heard that Lady Mac has married again, but it apparently has not worked out. During work on *Isn't Life Wonderful?* she calls Snitch and wants to see him. He visits her at the Netherland Hotel. She asks him to lend her $500, which Snitch feels unable to do. We presently learn that Mr. Frisbee has also remarried. He engages Snitch for a new task: to remove from *Heart of Africa* all scenes showing Lady Mackenzie.[21]

After *That Royle Girl* Snitch has a try at independent production, shooting a low-budget comedy short about a dog, titled *A Short Tail*. It wins him a contract for a series of such "novelty films" to be shot in Hollywood and released through Paramount. The first is well received—Snitch has the satisfaction of seeing it at Grauman's Egyptian Theatre—but on subsequent films Snitch disagrees with his backers and the project comes to a halt. Then Snitch falls ill and has major surgery, after which he is nursed back to health in Hollywood by none other than "Mother Carr" of *Over the Hill to the Poor House*. There is no mention of what has happened to Mr. Carr.

Returning to Maimie, Snitch gets an offer from Eastman Kodak, which wants to send him to India to introduce Panchromatic film there. He spends two years, 1928 to 1930, in India, building laboratories, training technicians, and indoctrinating major Indian film directors in the use of Panchromatic. When he leaves, Panchromatic film is "selling like wildfire."

Later he is engaged by Carveth Wells, lecturer and explorer, to accompany him as cinematographer on a 6,000-mile journey through the Soviet Union, and later through other countries. After that he joins the Commission on Cartography of the Pan American Institute of Geography and History, and stays with it for twenty years.

Thus a career in cinematography comes to a gradual close. But the diary habit is strong and entries continue, though in the end they may say little more than: "With Maimie, watched the Ed Sullivan Show."

NOTES

1. Upton Sinclair, *Upton Sinclair Presents William Fox* (Los Angeles: Sinclair, 1933), p. 59.

2. For Urban's role in the British film world and his troubles over Kinemacolor, see especially Rachael Low and Roger Manvell, *The History of the British Film, 1806–1906* (London: Allen & Unwin, 1948); Rachael Low, *The History of the British Film, 1906–1914* (London: Allen & Unwin, 1949); and Rachael Low, *The History of the British Film, 1914–1918* (London: Allen & Unwin, 1950). Although British usage would call for "colour," Urban followed American usage with "Kinemacolor."

3. Low, *British Film, 1914–1918*, lists a London Film Company that operated from 1913 to 1921, and a Union Film Publishing Company that operated from 1912 to 1914 using a converted skating rink as its studio.

4. Founded in Flushing, New York, in 1910, the Solax Company moved to Fort Lee in 1912 and was prominent throughout the teens. See Paul C. Spehr, *The Movies Begin: Making Movies in New Jersey, 1887–1920* (Newark: Newark Museum, 1977), pp. 80–84.

5. Launched in 1913, the Universal newsreel continued under various names until 1967. U. K. Whipple was one of its first three cameramen. Raymond Fielding, *The American Newsreel, 1911–1967* (Norman: University of Oklahoma Press, 1972), p. 105.

6. At first known only as "the Biograph Girl," Florence Lawrence defected to the IMP Company under her own name—a key event in the rise of the "star system."

7. *The Moving Picture World* (June 9 and 16, 1917). John Ernest Williamson's pioneering work in underwater photography is recounted by him in his autobiography: John Ernest Williamson, *Twenty Years under the Sea* (Boston: T. R. Hale, 1944).

8. The Houdini 1920 feature film *Terror Island* had an underwater climax involving a treasure chest (the heroine was locked in it but was rescued

by Houdini), which may have owed something to the Williamson-Sintzen-ich association.

9. The United States had declared war on April 6, 1917.

10. The space was later used by Edwin Armstrong for the invention of frequency modulation.

11. Better known to a later generation as director of *The Wizard of Oz* and *Gone with the Wind*, both released in 1939.

12. Alan Crosland later played a role in the advent of sound as director of *Don Juan* (1926) and *The Jazz Singer* (1927).

13. "It cost $100,000 to make, and netted over $3,000,000." Sinclair, *Upton Sinclair Presents William Fox*, p. 59.

14. Mary Carr (1874–1973) scored a success in 1919 in *Mrs. Wiggs of the Cabbage Patch* and went on to decades of mother roles, including a role in *Friendly Persuasion* (1956). She has been described as "the archetypal white-haired old mother." Leslie Halliwell, *The Filmgoer's Companion* (New York: Hill and Wang, 1977), p. 129.

15. J. G. Wilhelm ("Billy") Bitzer was D. W. Griffith's chief cameraman during his rise to fame and worked on *The Birth of a Nation, Intolerance, Way Down East*, and most other major Griffith works.

16. Mae Marsh had appeared in Griffith's *Man's Genesis, The Birth of a Nation*, and *Intolerance*. The new film, *The White Rose*, was her final Griffith appearance.

17. Actor and songwriter, composer of the World War I success "Keep the Home Fires Burning," Ivor Novello impressed Griffith with his resemblance to Richard Barthelmess, with the result that Griffith brought him to the United States.

18. Karl Brown, an earlier Griffith cameraman, described the competitive atmosphere among cameramen working with the master. The advent of Sartov, who specialized in misty close-ups, had "burned Bitzer to a crisp, which was what Griffith wanted," according to Brown. "But that was Griffith's way. Keep everybody in hot competition with any and all possible rivals." Karl Brown, *Adventures with D. W. Griffith* (New York: Farrar, Straus and Giroux, 1973), pp. 205–7.

19. Carol Dempster, pretty but with limited talent, appeared in a number of Griffith features during the last decade of the silent era. Griffith seemed determined to turn her into "another Lillian Gish or Mae Marsh." William K. Everson, *American Silent Film* (New York: Oxford University Press, 1978), p. 180.

20. For the complex maneuvers, see Robert M. Henderson, *D. W. Griffith: His Life and Work* (New York: Oxford University Press, 1972), pp. 246–53.

21. Referring to the success of *Heart of Africa*, Kevin Brownlow writes:

"Lady Grace Mackenzie was hailed as the first woman ever to penetrate so far into the jungle and was said to have outdone Rainey and Roosevelt. Mackenzie Camp in Kenya was named after her. But she ran into financial trouble, and both her business management and her title came under suspicion. A lawsuit ended her courageous but brief excursion into pictures." Kevin Brownlow, *The War, the West, and the Wilderness* (New York: Knopf, 1979), p. 415.

Berenice Abbott's photo of Wall Street showing the East River from the roof of the Irving Trust Building, 1938. In 1929 Berenice Abbott, already celebrated for a book of Paris photos, was planning a similar book on New York. The WPA made its completion and publication possible in the 1930s. In 1997 it was republished in a definitive edition by The New Press. (© *Museum of the City of New York*)

6

The Place to Be

IT WAS A SUNDAY AFTERNOON in the summer of '29, a few weeks post-Princeton. In New York I had begun a $30-a-week job at TIME, Inc. But this being Sunday, I had used the Columbia University tennis courts for a brisk two sets. (My father was a Columbia professor so I had tennis privileges.) Now, sweaty in my tennis clothes, I returned to the family apartment on Claremont Avenue, where I found Archie on duty on the elevator. I generally chatted with Archie on the way to the eleventh floor. Stretching and moaning a bit, I said, "Whew, I feel stiff."

Archie said, "I'm going to be stiff tonight."

"Oh? How so?"

"Going to a party. Friend of mine, named Clint. Gives great parties."

Archie seemed to want to tell more. "He's an intellectual. Has a private income. He owns an apartment house, and uses one of the apartments. So he gives these great parties."

"That should be nice for you."

"Would you like to go?"

"You mean to the party?"

"Sure. I can bring people. Any time."

"You sure?"

"Absolutely."

Archie had never before made such a suggestion. It seemed odd but it piqued my interest. Almost all my Princeton friends had been on Harlem pilgrimages, usually to places like the Cotton Club or other night spots. It was a thing to do—or at least, to have done. A rite of passage. I had never managed it—my allowance was not set with nightclubs in mind. But this was different, anyway. Not a tourist thing but a private event. Someone's home. It gave me some sense of one-upmanship vis-à-vis fellow Princetonians. I asked Archie, "You're sure it would be all right?"

"Absolutely."

"Well— I'd like to."

"Good. Meet me a little after midnight, in front of the building here. I'll have a taxi ready."

After midnight? That gave me pause. I supposed that was a normal starting time for a Clint party. But I had work to do next morning—which might be crucial. TIME, Inc. had put me on a new project—a magazine to be called *Fortune*. It would not debut until 1931 but meanwhile a staff was in place, getting assignments and turning out articles that went, for the moment, into the files instead of to press. We were on a shake-down cruise. Each of us had on our desk a handsome dummy copy of the magazine-to-be. It had many blank pages but also the beginnings of sample articles, along with lavish photographic layouts, so we could all sense the kind of publication we were aiming at. (The dummies were also, I assumed, used to sell future advertising.) I already had my assignment for next day, and it sounded great. I was to rendezvous at the TIME office with one Berenice Abbott, a photographer who had just arrived from Paris with a startling reputation. She had been an aide to the avant-garde artist and photographer Man Ray, and then become an apprentice—and disciple—to the celebrated Eugène Atget. Under his influence she had begun to document Paris—not the tourist Paris but *her* Paris, full of meaningful details that most people never saw. Never once had she pointed her camera at the Eiffel Tower. Her book of Paris photographs had created a stir. Now she had arrived in New York and apparently *Fortune* had plans for her, just as it had latched onto Margaret Bourke-White. It was another indication of where *Fortune* was headed. Anyway, I was to meet Abbott at 10 A.M. and together we were to taxi to the Brooklyn docks to meet the incoming luxury liner *Bremen* on her maiden voyage—an event with many ramifications. With this ship—sleek, speedy, deluxe—Germany was seen making its bid to recapture a share of Atlantic tourist traffic, lost because of the 1914 Great War and the ignominious postwar years. Germany, it was said, was now regaining its footing. The *Bremen*, reportedly a masterpiece, could be a major step. Some thought it might challenge—and break—the transatlantic speed record. All such talk gave an edge to my expedition with Berenice Abbott.

To jeopardize such an assignment for a Harlem party given by a mysterious Clint seemed preposterous. On the other hand, to attach such importance to a few hours' sleep seemed equally unworthy. At 12:03 A.M. I was at the apartment house door for Archie. A taxi stood ready. Twenty minutes later, somewhere near Lenox Avenue in Harlem, we arrived in front of a small apartment house and walked up to the second floor. A mighty buzzing, mingled with music, guided us and welcomed us in. We found ourselves in a large room crammed with people. A few were dancing.

One of the first things I noticed about Clint's apartment was the lighting. Every light bulb seemed to be amber. This made it difficult to see who was black and who might be white. It seemed a useful social gambit. Dominating the room as we entered was Clint (That *must* be Clint!), a large, ebullient man at a punchbowl, surrounded by an audience, officiating—creating what he called a cocktail, proclaiming its recipe as he proceeded. Into a layer of gin he deposited . . .

"Mission Orange!" he sang out, as the watchers cheered and the liquid splashed down. Then . . .

"Apricot brandy!" Clint had other bottles ready and they followed, each with its celebratory sendoff.

A bystander commented, "When Clint mixes a cocktail, he mixes his *whole* personality into that cocktail."

With drinking, and some dancing, and chatter, time passed quickly. Archie was having a high time and left me to my own devices. I got in a number of dances and enjoyed them. The style was different from what one saw at Princeton proms. The lady linked her hands around the man's neck, leaving little for him to do but link his around her waist. I rather liked this. The room was so crowded that couples did their dancing mainly in place, shuffling a bit to the music while shouting small talk. About 3 A.M., worrying about the *Bremen* and Berenice Abbott and *Fortune* magazine, I decided on a getaway. I made my way to Clint, thanked him for his hospitality, waved goodbye to Archie, and left. I sensed the party had hours to go. On Lenox Avenue I was able to find a taxi, and I got home about 4 A.M. I tried to sleep for a couple of hours, not too successfully. At six o'clock I got up, shaved, had a shower, and fixed some breakfast. I felt anything but spry. I took the subway downtown, changing at Times Square for the shuttle. Shortly before 9 A.M. I was at the TIME office, which was then on 42nd Street near Lexington Avenue. Berenice Abbott was already there, with all her gear. I was relieved that I was on time. I was determined to hold myself together for the next few hours.

I was given a cash advance for taxi money and incidentals. I was apparently in charge, financially speaking. The taxi trip to Brooklyn took almost an hour. My eyelids were so heavy that I feared I would doze off. But the excitement of the job slowly took hold and tided me over. After a time I no longer felt tired. Berenice Abbott was pleasant company. Not beautiful but poised, unpretentious, she seemed totally intent on the job at hand. She asked questions about places en route. She kept looking around, drinking in everything. She hoped in future weeks to chronicle, with her camera, the present moment in New York history. A city in rapid change. Glimpses of old New York, of decay, juxtaposed with the new rising out of the rubble. All this exhilarated her.[1] I got in the spirit and decided I would survive. Finally we arrived at the *Bremen*. The rakish curve of her prow, where it split the waters, was astonishing. We checked with the North German Lloyd "P.R." people, who gave me a sheaf of handouts, full of statistics, history, and so on. Finally we were aboard, moving from deck to deck, exploring wherever we could. She took shot after shot, rapidly but not hurrying. Every shot was carefully planned. She was forever looking around, weighing alternatives, vistas, where to place the camera. At one point I suggested a vista I found interesting—feeling, as I did so, that I shouldn't. It was an impertinence on my part. She said, "You have a good eye"—pleasing me immensely. We ate lunch on board, then worked two hours more. Occasionally I remembered how tired I was but she kept on, relentlessly. Finally we were ready to leave. We found a taxi and were on our way, back to TIME.

In the taxi, at long last, she seemed to wilt a bit. She put her head back, closed her eyes and said, "Forgive me if I fall asleep. I hardly had any sleep last night. A friend took me to a party up in Harlem. Crazy thing to do."

I asked, "Somewhere near Lenox Avenue?"

"Yes. Why do you ask? Some man called Clint. A great party giver, apparently. I got to bed about five. Crazy thing. But Harlem—I didn't want to miss that." She murmured again, "Crazy. . . ." A moment later she seemed sound asleep.

NOTE

1. This became *Changing New York*, which the New Press published in a magnificent edition.

Erik Barnouw in 1928 at the entrance to Camp-
bell Hall dormitory at Princeton University.
(*Author's collection*)

7

Radiator-Pipe Broadcasters

HERE'S A CAMPUS MYSTERY that has happened at a number of colleges, and is likely to happen at more. The dean, in his home at the edge of the campus, is tuning in the late-night news. Twisting his dial he suddenly finds a very loud radio station he never knew about, playing Sibelius's Second Symphony. It's so loud the dean is sure it's near by, but he finds nothing about it in his newspaper.

Then as the music ends an immature voice pipes up: "This is the student broadcasting station of ——— College, bringing you ———."

The dean is the man who gets another gray hair when anything "serious" happens on the campus. And this is serious. The dean knows that to operate a radio station you need a license from the Federal Communications Commission. To operate without a license is a Federal offense. He knows also that the FCC would hardly give a license in the standard-wave band to college students.

After the campus detectives, with the aid of a portable radio, have located the student broadcasters and brought them next day to the dean's office—well, then the fun begins. Because now the students, calmly and confidently, launch into language that no dean, in any of the forty-odd colleges where students are now broadcasting or pre-paring to broadcast, has quite been able to comprehend.

For a college dean is not likely to be an electrical wizard, capable of keeping up with a freshman. His education and experience just didn't equip him for that. He is not likely to understand how the radiator pipes of a university can be turned into a transmitting an-tenna; or how the college electric wires, or the water pipes, or the gas pipes, or the metal frameworks of buildings, can be used for the same purpose; or how this student invention makes it possible to run a radio station that works like a radio station but that, for technical reasons, isn't a radio station in the eyes of the Federal Communica-tions Commission—and therefore doesn't need a license.

First published in the *Saturday Evening Post*.

In layman's language, the FCC doesn't apply its regulations to any transmitter that broadcasts a very short distance, because if it did, it would have to apply them to a number of gadgets in which it is not interested. Wireless phonographs and remote-control-tuning devices are really miniature transmitters that broadcast across the room to your own radio. The distance these gadgets are allowed to radiate varies with the wavelength, but, in general, anything that broadcasts fewer than two hundred feet is safe from Federal interference.

Campus Air Waves

Two hundred feet is not very much, and that's where the radiator pipes, and so on, come in. Except for this added bit of ingenuity, the student station is simply a normal, though "flea-powered," radio station. It has one or two "studios" with microphones, a control booth or control desk, turn-tables for playing recordings, and a small transmitter of two to ten watts. Only Harvard uses more power— thirty watts. But in most cases the wattage used would hardly service one building, except for the fact that the basement transmitter is connected to the heating pipes, electric system, metal framework of buildings or any ready-made metal network, which thereby becomes the antenna of the transmitter. Anyone with a radio within a short distance of the transmitter or of the metal network being used as antenna, can pick up the station. Thus a large campus can be covered, even though the radiation of any part of the transmitting system keeps well within the legal two hundred feet.

There are several variations of the system. Sometimes wires through the campus underground tunnels connect the transmitter separately to the heating pipes or steel frameworks of each dormitory. Sometimes several dormitories are given miniature booster transmitters. Each campus has its own, slightly different solution.

Most college authorities hardly comprehend these mysteries, but are gradually beginning to realize that the students are right—that the radiator-pipe broadcasting station, invented and developed entirely by undergraduates, is legal, practical, and an invention holding exciting possibilities.

More than a year ago the campus broadcasters formed the Intercollegiate Broadcasting System, referred to familiarly as the I. B. S., and promptly held at Brown the first annual convention of the I. B.

S. The I. B. S. has set up a plan for the exchange of recorded programs among member stations. It has issued bulletins of technical advice for students in other colleges, and has thus inspired young men from coast to coast to start crawling through heating tunnels, climbing on roofs and going through the other preliminaries to going on the air. Campus stations are now breaking out like a rash across the map of America.

Some of the stations started with permission of college authorities, and some didn't. Some of the pioneers tried to get permission, but found it difficult to get the authorities to understand what it was all about. Deans were usually afraid someone would get an electric shock. In some colleges students just went ahead, and let the authorities find out about it. It was easier to get them to accept a *fait accompli* than to understand a diagram.

But those days are quickly passing. It may be a while before the deans and the presidents understand the technical side of it, but the early skepticism is gradually turning to enthusiasm. In several recent cases the colleges have contributed substantial sums to the student projects. The stations are student-run, with little or no faculty supervision. Even where the college has given financial help, it usually hasn't interfered with operation. So the stations have become student activities corresponding closely to the college newspapers.

The students generally divide themselves into programming, technical and administrative staffs. In programming, there is a heavy reliance on recorded music, popular and classical. Broadcast descriptions of basketball and football and other games are handled successfully via special wires. There are usually debates and campus forums. Another type of program that springs up on most campuses is the broadcasting of a prom or fraternity house party. The music of the dance is carried for several hours, with much interviewing of the more glamorous girls through a microphone carried around the dance floor.

The period from 5 to 6 P.M. is generally a swing period. Most students are in their rooms then and not in the mood for study. "Jive at Five" is the Wesleyan name for this hour. Harvard has a swing period that it calls "Jazz Lab."

Classical music is surprisingly popular. The students have generally requested more of it, especially for the late evening. There is some question whether most students actually listen to it or find it an effective background for study.

Buttering Up the Faculty

Professors are invited for talks and informal interviews—and respond with enthusiasm. A few universities have for years run licensed "educational" stations, but those have often been stuffy and not too popular. Professors usually prefer to talk on the student-run stations. There they feel more comfortable, and less as if they are auditioning one of their lectures for the college prexy. At Wesleyan one instructor made quite a hit reciting horror tales with music and sound-effect backgrounds.

Most of the stations run dramas intermittently. The Harvard boys ran a series of plays on the college and its history, one of which was called *Lo, the Butter Stinketh.*

The students have, on the whole, been very conservative about what they broadcast. The Harvard station caused Dean Chase some anxiety when it broadcast an interview with Ann Corio, burlesque star, on the art of the strip tease. But in general the students have been highly moral, and frequently invited their college presidents to speak over their facilities. It's good policy.

How large and how faithful is the listening audience of the student station? Though no authoritative survey exists, interest seems to be high. The campus broadcasters are pleasantly amazed at this. A feeling of grave responsibility descends on them. Above the announcer's desk at WES, Wesleyan, manager Robert Stuart has posted this sign: "When you give the time be accurate. *Guys set their watches by us!*"

A campus station is often born in one dormitory room. Princeton's station WPRU, small but swanky, has its home in the room of H. Grant Theis, '42, its creator and builder. The transmitter is in the basement of the same building. Amid the severe modernity of this radio studio there is only one grotesque touch—a bed. Theis could literally get into bed, yawn good night to his radio audience, turn a switch to shut off his station, turn over and go to sleep. Next to Theis's room is a small storeroom used as a continuity-writing room. There is just room for four continuity writers to sit in a row.

The Original Brown Network

In addition to broadcasting from his room, Theis's outfit can originate programs at various points on the campus to which he has underground lines. These include the gym and one classroom building. In the basement the station is connected with the university power lines, which carry the programs throughout the campus.

Wesleyan's station, less natty but in a more complex stage of development, has two studios and a control room in the basement of a dormitory. Brown has studio space that was donated by the university, in Faunce House, a building devoted to student activities. The Harvard station, which was started and financed by the *Harvard Crimson*, campus newspaper, shares quarters with the *Crimson*. But most stations start in somebody's room. The founder of the Dartmouth station used to blow a whistle out his window to announce he was about to go on the air.

All the stations have tales of unexpected catastrophes. It never occurred to Theis, at Princeton, that the phone in his room might ring just as he got on the air. It did, the first day. Somebody quickly removed the receiver, but didn't answer it till the end of the broadcast.

The Princeton station was built with about five hundred dollars in capital, chipped in by a small group of students. Some of the stations were started with a good deal less.

The history of how this perfectly legal form of bootleg broadcasting was invented is the story of two young geniuses of Brown University. George Abraham and David W. Borst were freshmen in 1936, and that's when it all started. By now both have graduated. David Borst has been hired by General Electric, and works in Schenectady; George Abraham, now a graduate student in physics at Harvard, is at the same time serving the international short-wave station WRUL, in Boston. Both remain active advisers of the Intercollegiate Broadcasting System.

As freshmen, living in different dormitories, they decided they wanted a system for communicating with each other. Each got a microphone and by running wires between the two dormitories arranged a speaking system that utilized the loudspeakers of their radios.

Other freshmen wanted to join this wired communication system.

Borst and Abraham arranged it at a charge of one-dollar per new member. Presently thousands of feet of wire were strung around the campus. The new members did not have microphones, and didn't need them. Borst and Abraham arranged it so that every member could talk to every other member simply by shouting into his own radio loudspeaker.

The system whereby everybody could shout at everybody else became a nuisance, and was gradually changed into one in which "broadcasts" were put on from Abraham's room, with the other rooms becoming listening posts. Each dormitory had a section manager who was supposed to keep the wires in his dormitory in repair, but this was a hopeless job, because maids with mops and brooms were constantly breaking them. Besides, the college authorities objected to so much wiring.

Time Out for Exams

So the boys evolved the system of a number of tiny transmitters, linked by underground wires, but not needing to be wired to the individual radios. Until now the system had merely been one of wired communication. Now it became radio. The next step was the utilizing of a ready-made metal network as antenna, for better coverage.

The system had already become known as the Brown Network. Other colleges, following suit, have called their systems "networks" rather than "stations." Wesleyan acquired a Cardinal Network, Harvard a Crimson Network, and the University of Connecticut a Husky Network.

A campus station, or network, just picks for itself the choicest open spot on the dial, usually right between two popular commercial stations. The students operate fairly limited schedules. Four P.M. to midnight, with an hour's intermission for dinner, is a typical day's program. A few colleges broadcast an alarm-clock program for an hour in the morning. During vacations and exams, and sometimes during weekends, they just stop broadcasting.

In a few colleges several rival stations have sprung up. This has been true at Swarthmore, Yale, and Wesleyan. At Wesleyan, Station WES had after a long battle won the approval of college authorities. When it was in full operation another station, without approval, started to broadcast. WES didn't mind this until the new station started to broadcast on WES's frequency, during hours when WES was not on. What's more, the new outfit started to run risqué records, of which WES had never been guilty. Some listeners, not knowing they were listening to a second station, blamed it on WES. Then WES got sore and did some protesting of its own. Then the authorities squelched the newcomer.

A more prevalent battle is over the question Shall we or shall we not sell advertising? At Harvard, the boys who put on Ann Corio are very much against commercialization. Other college stations have gone commercial, not as a money-making scheme, but to pay expenses and buy more and better equipment.

During the early days of the Brown Network, college authorities forbade the inventors to go ahead. At Wesleyan the station was held to violate a rule against musical instruments or "any disturbance likely to interfere with studies of others after 7:30 P.M." Authorities at both colleges soon changed their minds and gave permission, nervously at first.

The Brown students kept getting friendly but worried letters from the dean's office: "It has been pointed out to me that the Brown Network probably presents a fire hazard. I wish it would be possible for you to come to my office and persuade me that this is not so."

The boys did. Two years later, the Music Department of Brown University started to give academic credit to students who listened to the classical music programs of the station.

The change is significant. College authorities are beginning to realize that these stations, precisely because they are student activities, are an invaluable educational medium. Thus at Columbia, when the students asked for permission, they not only got permission but a gift of money to build a studio on their own specifications. Many colleges are now giving their student broadcasters this kind of encouragement and support.

At Columbia the students discussed the idea of having a late-evening program entitled "Music to Study By." Some students thought the faculty wouldn't like it, but when the idea was mentioned to a professor of educational psychology at Teachers College, he said: "Wonderful! Most students study with music anyway. Here's our chance to find out about it. Somebody here should do some research on that! We'll find out if music increases or decreases studying efficiency. Also, what kind of music is best. This is fine! Here's a chance for some real practical research!"

So the radiator-pipe station is going right ahead, winning student, dean, prexy and professor.

8

Mr. Greenback
Goes to Town

ANNOUNCER: "Mr. Greenback Goes to Town". . . presented by the Minute Men of the Greater New York War Bond Pledge Campaign . . . and starring Ezra Stone.
(MUSIC)
(APPLAUSE)
EZRA: Hello everybody. This part I'm playing today is different from anything I've done before. You see, I'm supposed to be a dollar bill. The story is the confessions of a greenback. I'm going to tell you all about my travels—all the people who have owned me, and what they did with me. I may have smothered in *your* wallet or handbag at one time. So listen to my side of it. . . .
(MUSIC CONTINUES BEHIND)
. . . My name is William Greenback . . . but just call me Bill. I'm not a very old dollar bill, though I've been through an awful lot in my time. It was only a few months ago that I was coming off the presses. And I'd like to tell you about that. I'd like you to know how that feels. Thousands of clean young bills marching off the press together out into the world. It's kind of solemn really. Kind of inspiring. Sort of like an Annapolis commencement, or like *any* commencement. All of us young and hopeful and idealistic, anxious to do our part to benefit mankind. Of course there wasn't any commencement speech for us, but if there had been, I think old Uncle Sam would have addressed us like this . . .
UNCLE SAM: Now as you greenbacks go out into the world, I want you to realize what you're going into. It's a mixed world with all kinds of people. Sometimes you'll be in the hands of fine men and women, who will use you worthily, and sometimes you'll be in hands that waste you. Then you'll feel your lives are futile, and that's a terrible feeling. Now as you go out there, with the diploma of Uncle Sam tattooed upon your chest, I want you to do all you can *not* to

lie idle. Speak up to whoever owns you, and say: "There's a dollar bill in your pocket that's crying to be used for good! Use me!" In some cases they won't hear you. But in others their conscience *will* hear you. So good luck. You're passing into a world that needs you badly, and needs all the good that you can do. I now graduate serial numbers W8734879B to W87349246L . . .

EZRA: Well, that's the spirit in which we left Washington, D.C., taking a last farewell look at our Alma Mater. Now, I won't tell you all the hands and pockets I passed through. . . .

(MUSIC SNEAK IN)

. . . I was in a bank for a while; then I was in the cashier's drawer of a soda fountain, and then in the handbag of a lady who had just bought a maple walnut sundae with whipped cream and a maraschino cherry. I well remember that handbag. There were many other bills in with me, and I was right next to a fifty-dollar bill who had a very superior expression. However, finally I spoke to him . . .

(MUSIC UP BRIEFLY AND OUT)

. . . My, it's close in this bag.

50: Very stuffy.

EZRA: And what a smell!

50: Very strong perfume.

EZRA: I don't like this. Where's this dame taking us, anyway?

50: I believe we're going into a beauty parlor now.

EZRA: A beauty parlor? Well, then I'm not doing any good! I wanna do good!

50: Take it easy.

EZRA: Why should I take it easy? There's a war going on! I want to do my part!

50: Relax.

EZRA: I don't like this . . . Ouch! What was that. Something stuck me.

50: She just put us down on a table. Probably a hairpin poked into you.

EZRA: It was her lipstick! And now I've got goo all over me!

50: You'll get marked up plenty before long.

EZRA: And I was so clean and crisp.

50: You'll be wilted soon enough.

EZRA: Like you, you mean?

50: My dear fellow, I am a very experienced fifty-dollar bill. I've bought some fine jewelry in my time. I've paid for several handsome radios. I bought a washing machine once. And I helped make a down payment on a sixteen-cylinder limousine.

EZRA: Oh, that's all prewar stuff. Nobody cares about that now. I don't want to be used for things like that!

50: You're just a young idealist. You'll get over it.

EZRA: I don't like your attitude. These aren't the palmy days any more. This is a crisis!

50: Typical young idealist. If you'd knocked around as long as I have, you'd realize this lady is probably going to use us both right here in this beauty parlor.

EZRA: What! You shock me! Shsh. Let's hear what's going on.

(ON FILTER)

LADY: Now, François, I want a permanent, and I want a facial too, and a manicure of course.

FRANÇOIS: Yes, Madame.

LADY: And I want everything very specially good.

FRANÇOIS: I understand, Madame.

LADY: I think it's so important nowadays, don't you? I mean for women to take care of their appearance, and to look just as feminine and gay as possible.

FRANÇOIS: Very important, Madame.

LADY: I mean particularly now with this dreadful war going on. I think we should be just as alluring and frivolous as possible, just to spite those terrible Nazis!

FRANÇOIS: Very good idea, Madame.

LADY: We're having a party this evening. We're having caviar canapes, with Daquiri cocktails. . . .

EZRA: Why this is terrible. Lady! Please! . . .

LADY: . . . Then jellied madrilene. Then filet of sole; with sauterne. . . .

EZRA: . . . Can't you hear me? . . .

LADY: . . . Then roast duck. With petitapois and mushrooms. . . .

EZRA: . . . Please! Use me. Put me to work for Uncle Sam.

LADY: . . . And champagne, of course. And then a relish. . . .

50: You young fool, she can't hear you.

LADY: . . . And to finish it off a baked Alaska, . . .

EZRA: She's got to hear me. Lady, please, it's important. . . .

LADY: . . . and of course coffee and portwine and liqueurs. . . .

EZRA: . . . You gotta listen. Please. Can't you hear me??
LADY: . . . I think it's so important, don't you?
50: Of course not. Relax.
FRANÇOIS: Oh yes, Madame.
LADY: I mean especially now. Now *especially*. We must be gay and civilized and do things just so. . . .
EZRA: Oh gosh. I'm being wasted. I'm being wasted. I'm a failure!
(MUSIC ON EZRA'S CURTAIN NO MATTER WHERE LADY HAPPENS TO BE)
LADY: . . . After all, it's the very civilization we're fighting for. . . .
(MUSIC FADES DOWN FOR NARRATION)
EZRA: Well, that was the beginning of the sorrowful period of my life. François used me in a gambling den, at a roulette table. The gambler used me in building up his hoard of alcoholic beverages. Wasn't that terrible? Why, if I'd met Mr. Morgenthau in those days, I couldn't have looked him in the face. I didn't dare look at the image of George Washington on my own chest. I felt awful. And all the time I kept trying to make those people hear me, trying to tell them how important it was. I remember one day, I was taken into an expensive sport store. I was in a man's wallet, and next to me was a twenty-dollar bill. . . .
(MUSIC UP BRIEFLY. OUT)
20: (sniffing) Say, I like the aroma of this guy's tobacco, don't you?
EZRA: Not bad.
20: It should be good. Six pieces of paper left this wallet to pay for his last can.
EZRA: I'm just itching to be used for a good cause. I feel I'm not keeping faith. Have you been made useful at all?
20: Oh, now and then. What's eating you, anyway? I suppose you're one of these new bills, just out from Washington.
EZRA: Yes, I guess I'm still a little green at it. But I'm aching to do good. Shsh. Let's hear what's up.
(ON FILTER)
MAN: Hmm. This is a rather nice sports jacket . . .
SALESMAN: It looks good on you, sir. Of course, so does this other one.
MAN: I'd better take them both.
SALESMAN: Yes, sir. That's . . . seventy-six dollars . . .
MAN: How much in all?

SALESMAN: Just four hundred and twenty-five.

MAN: Okay. Just charge it all and send it over.

SALESMAN: Yes, sir. Getting a nice long vacation, sir?

MAN: No. Just a couple of months.

(A SECOND'S PAUSE FOR EZRA'S WORDS)

EZRA: What? This is awful.

MAN: It's important these days, to get some relaxation. Particularly in times like these. We need it.

SALESMAN: Oh yes, sir.

MAN: Now let's see. The two bathing suits. The four pairs of white flannels. . . .

EZRA: (ON CUE: "flannels") Hey, Mister, please! Put me to work! Won't you use me for old Uncle Sam?

MAN: . . . Sweater. A dozen of those socks. The polo shirts and the neckties . . .

20: He won' t hear you.

MAN: . . . That's about all. Wait a minute, I'd better take another tennis racket and a couple more golf-clubs.

EZRA: What can I do? I'm desperate. I'm—I'm frustrated!

SALESMAN: Yes sir, right this way, sir.

(MUSIC ON EZRA'S CURTAIN LINE NO MATTER WHERE FILTERED DIALOGUE IS)

(MUSIC DOWN UNDER NARRATION)

EZRA: Now I don't want to give you the idea everybody was like that. I just happened to spend some of my early days being toted around by people with their minds set on luxuries. But finally the turning point came. I was in a frayed pocketbook of imitation leather, next to a five-dollar bill. I'd just been handed out as part of a payroll. The young man I was with then walked rapidly down the street. And next I heard . . .

(KEY IN DOOR. DOOR OPENING AND CLOSING)

(ON FILTER)

BOY: Darling.

GIRL: Johnny . . . Oh, I'm always so glad when you come home. It's the same way every day. It always has been, ever since we were married.

BOY: There's nothing I like better than coming home.

GIRL: At six o'clock I start watching for you. By half-past-six I'm so excited I can't stand it. And finally, when I hear your key in the door, my heart just jumps. I'm so happy. I . . . I've never read stories about people as happy as we. Is it really possible?

BOY: Not only possible, it's true. Kiss me.

EZRA: I like listening to stuff like this. Don't you?

5: Yeah. The girl sounds good looking, doesn't she?

EZRA: I'm sure she's a beauty. And she sounds like a nice, fine type of girl, too.

5: I bet she's a neat number.

EZRA: Shshh. (*pause*) (*whisper*) Long clinch, huh?

BOY: How's little Johnny?

GIRL: He's fine. He's just had his supper and gone to bed.

BOY: How was he today?

GIRL: Much better. His cold's almost gone. I think in a day or two he'll be his old self again.

BOY: Fine. Look, I got paid today. Ten dollars.

GIRL: That's good.

BOY: Here you are.

EZRA: (*sneezing violently; then sotto voce*) Sudden exposure always makes me sneeze.

5: Shsh.

BOY: Ten bucks.

GIRL: I'm glad you got it. The landlady said she'd simply have to have some money tonight.

BOY: All right, we'll put aside five bucks for her. That brings her up-to-date. . . .

EZRA: I guess you'll be leaving tonight, buddy.

5: Yeah. Well, that's life.

BOY: . . .Gosh, honey, you're good to stick by me, with me only earning ten bucks a week. If you ask me you're getting an awful deal.

GIRL: What are you talking about? How dare you say that? I think you're doing a wonderful thing, taking this part-time job, so you can go through all those technical courses, and really become valuable to the war effort. I think it's a marvelous thing, and as long as it's necessary I can make out on ten a week. I know I can.

BOY: Just the same, I wish I could buy you something fancy once in a while. And little Johnny too.

GIRL: Now don't talk like that. No one's happier than I am. And little Johnny's all right. We'll manage. Now look. If we set aside three-fifty for food for the week, I can make out. I've figured it out to the penny.

BOY: All right. That leaves one fifty. But don't we have to buy more of that medicine for little Johnny?

GIRL: Yes. That's fifty cents.

BOY: Okay. That leaves us one dollar.

GIRL: Well! We can practically splurge.

BOY: Gosh, you're wonderful! No kidding. What will we do with it?

GIRL: I don't know.

EZRA: (*speaking up*) How about some war stamps?

5: Shsh.

EZRA: (*sotto*) Well isn't that a good suggestion?

5: Leave them alone.

GIRL: I saw a shirt I'd like to buy you; you need a shirt, darling.

BOY: No, I don't want to spend it on that. I don't need a shirt for a while.

EZRA: (*up, impatiently*) Why not war stamps?

5: Shsh.

BOY: We could get you a hat or something. Or a pair of stockings. That's what *I'd* like to get with it.

GIRL: No, darling, I don't want to spend it on that.

EZRA: (*impatient*) What's the matter with war stamps????

5: Shshsh.

BOY: I saw some swell building blocks I'd like to get for little Johnny.

EZRA: Naww . . .

GIRL: I don't think we should do that. He plays very happily with pans and things around the kitchen. He's so cute.

EZRA: (*plaintive*) I still don't see what's wrong with *my* suggestion. Gosh, maybe they don't hear me.

BOY: We'd better just stick it away in a safe place. Save it for a rainy day. Hide it in the vase up on the shelf there.

EZRA: Aw, mister, please don't do that.

GIRL: Somehow, I'd rather not do that, Johnny.

EZRA: (*pleased*) Gosh, maybe she heard me.

5: Quiet.

GIRL: You know what I was thinking?

BOY: What?

GIRL: One dollar is just ten percent of your salary.

BOY: Yeah?

GIRL: Remember that campaign we heard about, in which they're trying to get everybody to lend ten percent of their salary to the government for the war effort?

BOY: But gosh . . . they don't expect people who only earn ten bucks to do that, do they?

GIRL: Maybe not. But if we could manage it, it would be wonderful. Just think, we could join the ten percent club.

BOY: But—one buck. That's an awful lot to us, and . . . what's one buck to the government?

GIRL: If several million give a dollar, it's an awful lot. Think of all they could do with that!

BOY: Yes, but . . . don't you think we ought to . . . put it away for an emergency?

GIRL: This is an emergency, Johnny. You've said that yourself. It's *our* emergency. We'd be doing it for *us*. Is there anything that means more to us than that Johnny should grow up in the kind of world that we believe in?

JOHNNY: When you put it that way . . . I guess there's nothing I'd rather do with this dollar. You're right, honey.

EZRA: Whoopee! She heard me!

(MUSIC, JUBILANT, UNDER NARRATION IT BECOMES A MARCH)

EZRA: Well, after that things sure started happening for me. I was in the war effort, and was I busy! I can't tell you all the times I've shuttled back and forth across this country . . . You see, when Johnny bought those war stamps, he handed me back to Uncle Sam to use. And Uncle Sam gave me to a factory that was making war planes for him. And so the first thing I paid for was a little piece of metal in the wing of one plane. And one day, over in China, that plane . . .

(SUDDEN FULL VOLUME AIRPLANE ROAR)

AVIATOR: All right, let 'em have it! . . .

(MACHINE GUN)

AVIATOR: . . . We got 'em. They're going down!

VOICE: Yeah, but look. We got caught through the left wing.

AVIATOR: We're all right. She'll hold.

(SOUND OUT)

EZRA: And she did hold. Cause that was *my* piece of metal that got hit. The piece of metal I paid for in that fine factory, that was working for Uncle. Well, after I'd got that plane on its way to China, the factory gave me to a workman on the payroll, and the workman joined the ten percent club and lent me back to Uncle Sam, and Uncle Sam gave me to a tank factory that was making him some tanks. And one day, over on the Russian front . . .

(TANK MOTOR. MACHINE GUN FIRE FROM DISTANCE)

TANKIST 1: All right. We'll charge that gun position. Ready. Go!

(TANK GETTING UNDERWAY)

TANKIST 2: They're hitting us square.

TANKIST 1: We'll make it! Keep going.

(TANK UP, SUDDENLY OUT)

EZRA: Now one of the places that tank was hit was a part that I'd paid for. But we held together and took that gun position! Meanwhile, back in the U.S.A., having helped pay for that tank, I was used on the factory payroll, and the man who got me bought a war bond, and so once more I was working for the government. Well, this time, I was used to help buy the motor for an aircraft rescue ship, and one day just recently, down in Australian waters . . .

(MOTOR BOAT AT HIGH SPEED BOUNCING THROUGH WATER)

SAILOR 1: Straight ahead! A man in the water . . .

SAILOR 2: I see him.

(SPEED UP A MOMENT, THEN SLOW DOWN AND STOP)

(WATERLAPPING SOUNDS STAY)

VOICE: (faintly) Help . . . help . . .

SAILOR 1: Hang on, sailor. We'll pull you out.

(SOUND OF EFFORT. WATER DRIPPING OFF MAN AS HE IS HAULED OUT OF WATER)

SAILOR 1: That's it. Take it easy, fellah.

VOICE: Had to bale out. All day . . . in the water . . . Couldn't have stayed afloat another minute. Thanks . . . thanks . . .

(WATER OUT)

EZRA: Well, it was the speed of that motor of mine, in that aircraft rescue ship, that saved that man. That's just a sample of the kind of thing I've been doing. Every time I go back to Uncle Sam, I buy something else. On the West Coast I paid for a seven-millionth part of a submarine . . .

VOICE 1: A one-dollar savings stamp, please.

EZRA: In the Middle West I bought a ten-thousandth part of one torpedo . . .

VOICE 2: I want to join the ten percent club.

EZRA: In the East I became one six-hundredth of a machine-gun . . .

VOICE 3: A war saving stamp—one dollar.

EZRA: And down South I launched a hundred-millionth of one battleship . . .

VOICE 4: I want to join the ten percent club.

EZRA: Boy, I've been busy. All over the place. Mrs. Roosevelt has nothing on me at all. . . . Now I'll admit that often, as I went from hand to pocket, and from pocket to payroll, and from payroll to tiller, in stores and factories and banks and mines, often I thought about Johnny, and his wife, and little Johnny, the ones who really started me on my useful life. The ones who first put me to work for victory. I often wondered if they'd made out okay. It sounded kind of like a tight squeeze to me, living on ten a week, and once in a while I worried about them. And so I was kind of happy when one day I suddenly found myself in a familiar wallet. That evening I pricked up my ears, and sure enough I heard familiar voices . . .

(MUSIC UP BRIEFLY WITH ROMANTIC STUFF, THEN DOWN AND OUT)

(ON FILTER)

GIRL: Oh darling, I'm so glad when you get home.

BOY: Look darling, I got paid again today.

EZRA: (*sudden big sneeze*) These sudden exposures—I can't get used to them.

GIRL: Fine. We can put aside a dollar for stamps, as usual, can't we?

BOY: You bet. Loyal members of the ten percent club. Here we are, one dollar for stamps . . . Say wait a minute.

GIRL: What's the matter?

BOY: That bill . . . I recognize it. I remember that funny streak of lipstick or something, in the corner.

EZRA: He recognizes me!

BOY: That's the bill I bought those first savings stamps with, when we joined the ten percent club.

GIRL: What a strange thing.

BOY: Boy, it sure looks different.

EZRA: Well, you can't look like a daisy after what I've been through. I've seen life!

BOY: I remember it was a new crisp bill, probably just off the presses.

But I'm sure it was the same one. That streak of lipstick was just that way.

EZRA: Right across George Washington's face too. I always felt bad about that.

GIRL: Darling, I just thought of something. That day, for a moment we talked about putting that dollar bill in that vase up there, and not using it. If we had, that bill would have still been new today, all crinkly and clean. But it wouldn't have done a bit of good all these months. It would have just sat there, being wasted. Instead of that, it's been in the service of Uncle Sam. Just think of all the things it may have done since we last had it. All the times it may have helped pay for arms and supplies to send our men abroad. It's awful to think we might have stopped it from doing that.

BOY: I'm glad we didn't.

GIRL: I am too. Look at that bill. It's a grizzled, battle-scarred veteran in the wars for Uncle Sam. Soldier, long may you circulate.

EZRA: Lady, God bless you for those words.

GIRL: God bless you, dollar bill.

EZRA: She heard me!

(MUSIC DOWN AS BACKGROUND TO:)

EZRA: She was right about what she said. I *am* a battle-scarred veteran. I've got some mileage left in me yet—but I know I'm a bit grimy looking. Unkempt—you know. I'm not like I used to be. Some day soon women will start handing me back to the grocer and saying . . .

WOMAN: Oh, what a dirty bill. Haven' t you got a cleaner one? Give me that other one, won't you?

EZRA: Me, a veteran of Uncle Sam's battles. But I know it must come. Some day they'll send me back to the Treasury. But—there's one thing I want to make clear. When Johnny and his wife decided to invest me in the future of a free world, they were thinking of the cause of all free people. But there's more to it than that. Because one day, just ten years from now, I'm going to come back to Johnny and his wife and little Johnny. Yes, I am. Oh, it may not be in my present incarnation. It'll probably be after I've gone back and been ground up and rolled and pressed into a new bill. Yes, I'll be all crisp again, and other bills will be green with envy. But then, ten years from now, I'll go back to Johnny. I like to imagine how it'll happen.

One evening, from the darkness inside a leather wallet, I'll hear familiar voices . . .
(MUSIC UP BRIEFLY. ROMANTIC OUT)
(ON FILTER)
GIRL: Dear . . .
BOY: Yes . . .
GIRL: Don't you think we ought to raise Johnny's allowance? Ten dollars a month isn't quite enough, at his age.
BOY: All right, sure. I'll see if I have some singles. I'll give him a little extra when he comes in. Let's see . . . one . . . two . . . three . . . four . . .
EZRA: (*big sneeze*) Achoooo. Hello. Remember me?
BOY: That ought to take care of him for a couple of dates.
EZRA: Don't you hear me?
GIRL: That's grand, dear. I'm glad you agree. (*sighing happily*) Oh, it's good to sit down in the evening.
BOY: Sure is. Want part of the paper?
GIRL: No darling. I'll just do my knitting.
EZRA: I guess you don't recognize me. Of course I know I look different, all glossy and reborn, and without that lipstick. But it's the same me. And not only that, but—What I really wanted to tell you was . . .
BOY: (OVERLAPPING WITH EZRA A WORD OR TWO) Say . . . who is this new girl Johnny's going out with? Where did he find her?
GIRL: I think he met her at some dance. She seems a nice quiet little thing. I think she's really all right.
BOY: Well—that's good.
EZRA: . . . What I wanted to say was—I haven't come back alone. I've brought thirty-three cents with me. And that's one reason why you can give your boy a little extra allowance now. Because every other dollar you put into war bonds has also come back with thirty-three cents. Yes, sir, that's the way Uncle Sam treats you. You lend him a dollar to defend your freedom, and he not only *does* defend it, but later he gives you back a dollar and thirty-three cents. That's pretty good. Still, I think you deserve it, 'cause you helped out when the going was tough. I'll always be grateful to you for that. (*pained*) Don't you hear me at all?
GIRL: I just thought of something.
BOY: What's that?

GIRL: Remember that room we used to live in when you were working at that part-time job, and how hard we worked to save one dollar a week?

BOY: Yeah. Seems a long time ago, doesn't it?

GIRL: I don't know why I suddenly thought of that.

EZRA: I guess in a way she did hear me.

(MUSIC TENDERLY. BACKGROUND TO:)

EZRA: Well, let's forget the future now, and come back to the present. Because the war's going on, and there's an awful lot of work to do. I expect to be hard at it for quite a while yet, back and forth across the country, helping with ships and planes and guns and tanks and pontoon bridges and whatnot. And here's what I'd like to say to you who've been listening to my autobiography: I may be in your pocket or wallet or handbag one of these days. And when I am I'll be saying as loud as I can: "There's a dollar bill in your pocket that's crying to be used for the service of Uncle Sam. Don't waste me! Put me to work for our country." Don't let me shout in vain, will you? Try to hear me.

Which reminds me: sometime between June 14th and June 24th a Minute Man will be ringing your doorbell. A Minute Man, going from door to door for Uncle Sam, to ask you if you'll pledge ten percent of your salary to the purchase of war bonds and stamps, just like my friends Johnny and his wife did. Your Minute Man doesn't want your money; he only wants your pledge. He just wants you to pledge to join the ten percent club; that is, the people who are lending ten percent of their income to their government for the drive to victory. Your Minute Man will give you a ten percent sticker, and ten percent buttons for every member of your family. Wear your button and display your sticker, because they mean, "I'm doing my share; I'm putting my quota, my ten percent into war bonds and stamps." Remember, you can get the sticker and the buttons from the Minute Man who will be ringing your doorbell soon. Ask him in; he's your friend. One minute with your Minute Man now means a lifetime of freedom. When he rings your doorbell, that's the liberty bell ringing. So have a talk with him. He'll tell you how important your dollar can be, or your ten dollars, or your fifty dollars, or your hundred dollars, or whatever your quota may be.

And, just to add a personal note to this, I'd like to say that to us bills, there isn't a better feeling than to be lying out flat on the counter of a bank or post office or some place, along with other bills, and to hear a voice up there saying:

VOICE: (ON FILTER) I want to buy a bond.

EZRA: Gosh that sounds good. Keep at it, folks. So long.

(MUSIC)

(APPLAUSE)

ANNOUNCER: This half-hour program was written especially for the Minute Men of the Greater New York War Bond Pledge Campaign by Erik Barnouw. We wish to extend our thanks to Ezra Stone . . . star of the Aldrich Family program and to Miss ———— who will soon be seen in the ———— picture ————.

The supporting players were ————, ————, ————, ————, ————, ————, ————, ————.

And the broadcast was made possible through the courtesy and cooperation of the Columbia Broadcasting System.

9

Kitty Sullivan and Social Security

NOTE: "Kitty" passages are excerpts from a tape-recorded interview, three reels in length. Numbers indicate reel in which material is to be found. Asterisks *** indicate where passages in the original interview must be eliminated by the tape editor.

EMERSON: Hello. This is Faye Emerson. I want to tell you about someone we'll call Kitty Sullivan. She works in the ladies washroom of an upscale restaurant. She's the washroom attendant . . . the matron. She hands people soap . . . a towel . . . maybe some hand lotion. She keeps the place looking tidy. When she started, she didn't think she would like the job. But she does, rather.

KITTY (2): I meet nice people. Some of them are not so nice, but then I think, "Well, they've got something on their minds, something worries them. And they just can't help it if they're not so gracious.". . . But on the whole, they're nice . . . polite. . . .

EMERSON: Once upon a time, Kitty studied law at New York University Law School. The ladies who come to Kitty's restaurant washroom, and perhaps tip her for her services, probably don't suspect anything like that. Because Kitty is old now . . . in her *eighties.* She's living on her social security, earning something extra with her work. . . . You see, when you're over seventy-two, you may earn as much as you're able, and *still* draw regular social security payments. It's a special incentive given to the old. And Kitty appreciates that, because she needs money for a *special project* of her own, that I'll tell you about later.

This is one of a series of programs called *Crossroads,* stories of people at certain great crossroads in their lives. These stories are brought to you by the Social Security Administration to help show how the law works in individual cases. I know this can be important to many of you, so I'm pleased to have been asked to narrate these stories for you.

Now let's get back to Kitty.

Her working life began, believe it or not, seventy-four years ago. She remembers it this way: it was just before President Garfield was assassinated . . . 1881.

KITTY (1): I went to work very young. Because in those days you could go to work as young as eight or nine years old. Some factories in the States, they took children as young as that . . . I worked in Stern's as a cash girl. *** And I got $1.50 a week. And then there was a rule that we could get $1.75 after three months and $2.00 after six months. But I was lucky in this . . . that when the three months were up, they decided to give us all $2.00, instead of waiting six months. And then while I was there . . . I was there nearly ten years and I knew the old firm Stern Brothers . . . and one year I helped in the lunch room a while and I got fifty cents extra for that, I think it was fifty cents extra a week for that. And then one day . . . Mr. Isaac Stern had been on a European trip . . . And when he came back, I went up to see him one evening. And I said, "Good evening, Mr. Stern, I am glad to see you back." Now I wasn't diplomatic . . . a *bit* diplomatic . . . because when he said, "Why?" *** I should have said, "Because it's nice to see you." But I wasn't a bit diplomatic, I am *not* a diplomat. I said, "Well, I would like to have more wages, more salary." Imagine that! After saying I was glad to see him back, instead of saying, "It's nice to have you back," or something like that. Well that's what I did. So then I told him that I had a mother and she had five children. I wasn't the oldest. My father had died about three years before, in about '78 I guess, and I was the oldest at home. Three brothers had got married, they had . . . Anyway, the result of that interview meant that I got $1.50 more a week. Wasn't that nice? So I was getting $4.50 instead of $3.00. Wasn't that nice? That was a nice increase! I never forgot that, how nice Mr. Stern was. See, he thought of the widow with her children and that I was helping. He was very lovely. . . .

EMERSON: And so Kitty was launched on a business career during the Presidency of James Garfield. She worked steadily year after year, but meanwhile she also studied, taking night courses. About the time President Benjamin Harrison came into office, Kitty got her high school diploma, through night courses. As Grover Cleveland entered the White House for his second term, Kitty was studying shorthand, and the still very new art of typewriting. This won her a job as secretary with a manufacturing firm. Then early in this century, Kitty took college courses at New York University and this led to a scholarship at the NYU Law School.

Kitty entered law school but never finished. Other matters claimed her time and earnings. Her younger sister, during these years, had grown up, married, had a daughter, and died. The husband had also died. Kitty's young niece was alone in the world. The year . . . 1911.

KITTY (2): Of course, the responsibility then fell on me. *** So I sent her to private school for her primary, almost all of her primary, and her high school, and her college . . .

EMERSON: Raising her niece, and giving her the best possible education, became Kitty's great adventure. Kitty's work as a secretary . . . nine to five, Monday to Saturday, year after year made the adventure possible. In 1922 the niece graduated from high school. In 1926, from college. Three years later the girl got married and before long had two children. But meanwhile . . . came the stock market crash.

It was hard for the young couple. But harder for Kitty. Her company went out of business. In her sixties, Kitty was out of a job. When the Social Security Law was passed in 1935, it meant nothing to her. Having no jobs, she wasn't covered. Then, at last, came a new chance . . . the washroom job.

KITTY (2): I got my present job because I prayed for something to do. I am a Catholic, and we have novenas in our church and I just finished a novena. And one morning . . . I generally went to church when I wasn't working, I mean on weekdays . . . one morning, I was on my way to church, and I thought before I go . . . I was early . . . that I'd stop in the Safeway, which is around the corner, to see if they had a certain kind of soup I wanted. I thought if they don't have it, then after church I will go to the A&P. *** And that's the first time I did that and that was the day after the novena finished. It was really most remarkable. It was the perfect answer to prayer. Nobody can tell me anything different. Because I had never been inspired to stop like that before and while we were there . . . there were two windows, and some people were on one side and some on the other. *** And the man . . . the safe was in the window . . . he was trying to open it and he was having difficulty. So this lady next to me said, "Well, I don't feel like waiting much longer, three of us have to go to work." And I said, *** "You might as well wait. I think he's getting it now." And so he was, he was getting it. So I told her that I was looking for work. *** So she said, "I probably shouldn't tell you this, but *** I want to help you." That's it, "I want to help you." Now, wasn't that nice of her?

EMERSON: The woman gave her information about the available job. When Kitty learned what kind of job it was, she hesitated. She waited three days.

KITTY (2): In fact, I didn't want to take it. I resented it. *** To think I should be a matron. I never thought of such a thing. So for three days I didn't go to see about it.

EMERSON: Then she heard that the job was still open. Perhaps, after all, she should apply. Kitty decided to go after it.

KITTY (2): I went there to the office. And the woman said . . . I told the woman, what I wanted . . . She gave me the application . . . I don't know whether I should tell this part, about the age business, but it's kind of interesting . . . So I said to her, when I came to date of birth on the application, "Do I have to tell my true age?" And she said, "Oh, I don't care what you put down." So I put down . . . oh, I put down a terrible difference! The same month and day, but *twenty* years difference. Twenty years . . . the nerve of me! My goodness. And then I didn't know I was putting myself in for social security. *** But when I got my first pay envelope, I saw they had taken off something for social security. "My goodness," I thought, "What have I done? I never thought of this!" I never thought of social security, date of birth. See, I never thought of that when I was putting down date of birth.

EMERSON: One of the things that worried Kitty was this: Would she be unable to collect any benefits for years and years, because of the misstatement?

KITTY: Oh yes, that was very important! I thought I wouldn't be able to collect until I was 65 according to the record that I gave the company. Imagine that!

EMERSON: On the advice of a friend, Kitty went to the Social Security offices to put the record straight. The files were corrected.

A few years later Kitty reached sixty-five. She could have retired and drawn small, regular retirement benefits, but she decided instead to keep working, and build up her social security account. You see, the benefits you finally get are determined in part by the payments that have been made to your account. So Kitty kept working year after year. She became reconciled to her job.

KITTY (2): During the day, I don't have to do the rough work. That's done before I come in . . . that is, the cleaning of the floor, the mirrors and such. That's all done because they have to be ready for customers when I get in. And then during the day, I keep the toilet covers nice and I keep the place tidy in case papers are thrown around. We have some paper towels, some linen towels. And the customers come in, if they have to come in to doll up. They come in at intervals, and I just wait for them. I sit down a good deal. I am up and down, and I have different kinds of people to wait on. Some of them are perfect ladies . . . perfect ladies. They always have their own cosmetics . . . always have their own cosmetics. They never have to ask me if I have powder or rouge, or . . . as one woman asked me the other day, if I had Vicks. I thought what on earth is this, have I come to be a drugstore? Vicks *** So I have hand lotion and I have a lot of other things . . . cotton, and Band-aids and various little things like that. *** The Band-aids they provide; the cotton and some of the things I provide myself. The hand lotions, I provide.

EMERSON: Today Kitty is in her eighties. She has built up her social security, and the payments she now draws are enough to support her. But she *still* keeps working! . . . Why? . . . I mentioned a while ago that she is financing a pet project, a new adventure, and this is it: her niece's two children are almost grown. Kitty has been helping to put them through college!

KITTY (2): And now her daughter, whom I provided for, is graduating from college in June. *** And her boy whom I'm providing for, who is already provided for . . . I put the money aside . . . is in first year college. And he'll finish college. So that's three college educations, and a home . . . a house, for my niece and her family. *** All that I paid for. But isn't it nice, it's awful nice, not to have money, but to feel that you've done something useful.

EMERSON: Kitty Sullivan, more than fifteen years a washroom matron, can feel a wonderful pride in what she has done. She says that social security took the fear out of old age; and that because of this, she felt no hesitation about the new adventure of her later days. And that explains why she feels as she does about social security.

KITTY(3): And it is better to work steady *** than to drop out like some people I understand do and collect unemployment insurance. It is much better to work steadily and get your social security built up, because that is for the future. The government's taking care of it. They invest it for you and you don't miss it, it is taken out each week and you know that it is coming back to you some time and at a time that is very important in your life. You may be very young and you think little of it, but don't let your youth hide the fact that the years are going on and that some time you will need your social security and it is lovely to have it. It's wonderful. It's a wonderful incentive, to work . . . to help. You feel that, well, you have that much and you can spend a little more maybe. *** At least you feel certain of a place to sleep, and something to eat. When you get to be sixty-five instead of going with your hat in your hand to some charity organization or to the police station and tell them that you haven't any place to stay, whereas you get your check every month and you are sure you will be accepted some place. *** And it makes us happy and more contented in our work, and if sometimes something disagreeable happens, we say, "Oh well, that was yesterday, forget about it. We are just going on, I am not going to throw up this job because of some ugly fellow in it . . . and maybe *I* am ugly too. I am just going to do the best I can and build up that social security because each day I lose, I lose social security, whereas if I work, I am building up a nice saving for the years when I can't work any longer."

EMERSON: Now here's a word from Mr. ———, of the Social Security Administration.

MR. ———: The case history you've heard shows several things I'd like to emphasize.

When you approach sixty-five, it's important to get in touch with your local social security office. Find out what retirement benefits you will be entitled to.

If you are able to work after sixty-five, you may in some cases be able to build up your account, and increase your later benefits.

Social security is saving many people anxiety at the crossroads of their lives. The system is paid for by tax contributions paid by your employer and you. If you have any questions about your rights or obligations under the law, inquire at your local social security office. If you don't know where it is, ask at the post office. Thank you.

(MUSIC: A PASSAGE OF 30–60 SECONDS, SUITABLE FOR BACKGROUND USE. LOCAL STATION CAN RUN AT FULL VOLUME, OR CAN FADE DOWN FOR ADDRESS OF LOCAL SOCIAL SECURITY OFFICE.)

EMERSON: This is Faye Emerson once more, inviting you to listen again to *Crossroads* . . . stories from the files of the Social Security Administration. The program was produced for Social Security by the Center for Mass Communication at Columbia University under the direction of Erik Barnouw.

"August 6 . . . The flash of the bomb made permanent shadows, burned into wood, etched into stone. Leaves, flowers, and men disappeared, but their shadows remained." A still from *Hiroshima-Nagasaki, August 1945. (Columbia University, courtesy of the author)*

10

Columbia and the
A-Bomb Film

EARLY IN 1968, while I was serving as chairman of the film division of the Columbia University School of the Arts, I received in the mail a clipping, dated January 26 of that year, from the English-language Japanese newspaper *Asahi Evening News*. It reported that the footage shot in Hiroshima and Nagasaki in 1945 by Japanese cameramen had finally been returned to Japan by the U.S. government. The Japanese government was said to be planning a television showing "after certain scenes showing victims' disfiguring burns are deleted." The footage would later be made available on loan to "research institutions," but: "In order to avoid the film being utilized for political purposes, applications for loan of the film from labor unions and political organizations will be turned down." This statement was puzzling to me for several reasons, but my main reaction was astonishment that such footage existed, since no one I talked to had been aware of its existence.

The clipping had been sent to me by a friend, Mrs. Lucy Lemann of New York City. I knew her as a frequent benefactor of the annual Robert Flaherty Film Seminars, which at that time were administered from Columbia and which I had helped organize. She was also a supporter of the World Law Fund, and at her suggestion I wrote for further information to Professor Yoshikazu Sakamoto, professor of international politics at the University of Tokyo, an associate of the Fund. His reply was that the Japanese had negotiated with the U.S. Department of State for return of the film but that the U.S. Department of Defense was thought to control it. The film sent to Japan was apparently not the original nitrate but a safety-film copy.

Somewhat impulsively, I wrote a letter on Columbia stationery as "Chairman, Film, Radio, Television" addressed to "The Honorable Clark M. Clifford, Secretary of Defense," with a notation that a copy should go to Secretary of State Dean Rusk and to Dr. Grayson Kirk, president of Columbia University. My inquiry was whether Columbia's Center for Mass Communication, a division of Columbia University Press producing and distributing documentary films and recordings, might have the privilege of releasing in the United States the material recently made available to Japan. I felt a bit flamboyant in all this, but sensed I had little to lose. Dr. Kirk promptly sent me a note expressing his support, and I was surprised to receive, within days, a reply from Daniel Z. Henkin, Deputy Assistant Secretary of Defense: The material had been turned over to the National Archives, and we could have access to it.

So it was that in April 1968 I sat in the auditorium of the National Archives in Washington viewing the two hours and forty minutes of footage. With me were film division associates and Mrs. Lemann. We also examined voluminous shot lists in which the location of every shot was identified and its contents summarized and cross-indexed. Every sheet bore the SECRET classification stamp, but this had been crossed out and another stamp substituted: "Not To Be Released Without Approval of the D.O.D." This partial declassification was not dated. Perhaps it had been a routine action taken without public announcement, or perhaps we were the first to have asked about the material.

Our group was staggered by some of the shots, and troubled by some aspects. The footage had been arranged in sequences under the overall heading "Effects of the Atomic Bomb." Effects on concrete, wood, foliage, internal organs, and so on were shown in separate sequences; scientific documentation had been the keynote. Effects on human beings were, however, only sparsely represented— although the few such shots were unforgettable.

A grant from Mrs. Lemann to Columbia University Press enabled us to order a complete duplicate of the footage—master positive, duplicate negative, and work-print copies. Late in 1968 this material began arriving at the Columbia campus from National Archives laboratories and we began a year of intensive work, selecting and rearranging the footage with constant reference to the priceless shot lists.

Troubled and puzzled by the paucity of "human-effects footage," as we began to call it, we wrote to the Defense Department asking whether material was being withheld from us. The Pentagon staff historian assured us that nothing was held back. He added: "Out-takes from the original production no longer exist, having probably been destroyed during the conversion . . . to safety film—if they were turned over to the U.S. Government at all." This curious reply made us wonder whether some of the original film was still in Japan, and we began voluminous letter-writing, inquiring about the possibility. The letters were addressed to Japanese documentarists and journalists and to Americans who had served in Japan during the occupation. Months of effort proved fruitless insofar as "human-effects footage" was concerned, but we did acquire American footage of the Hiroshima and Nagasaki blasts taken from the American observation planes, and footage of the Alamogordo test blast. The Hiroshima shot was acquired from Harold Agnew, who as a personal venture had taken his 16mm camera on the mission. His shot documented tellingly the shuddering impact of the blast on the observation plane itself, which seems for a moment likely to be blown to perdition. Harold Agnew later became head of the Los Alamos laboratories.

At this time we knew almost nothing of the history of the footage we were working with, nor of the men who had shot it. We knew from the Defense Department material that the film was the work of the Japanese documentary unit Nippon Eiga Sha, a wartime amalgamation of various pre-war Japanese documentary and newsreel groups, but the Defense Department had not provided individual credits. Unwittingly, in the course of our letter-writing, we had addressed an inquiry to the man who had headed the project for Nippon Eiga Sha: Akira Iwasaki, film historian and an occasional screenwriter and producer. He had made no immediate reply. Only later, after our film had been telecast in Japan (twice on prime time), did he get in touch with us and provide detailed information.

It took us almost a year to evolve the final pattern of *Hiroshima-Nagasaki, August 1945*. Our first rough assembly was some forty minutes long, but we kept shaving and rearranging passages for sharper impact. What finally emerged was a quiet sixteen-minute film with a factual, eloquently understated narration by Paul Ronder and spoken by him and Kazuko Oshimo. Ronder and Geoffrey Bartz did the editing. Both were students in the film division of the School of the Arts when the work began; by the time it was finished, Ronder had become an instructor and Bartz was on his way to becoming a highly successful film editor. Two music students, Linnea Johnson and Terrill Schukraft, improvised an unusual score featuring an oboe and a human voice—the latter used as a musical instrument, wordlessly.

Barbara Van Dyke of the Center for Mass Communication was associate producer. Professor of history Henry Graff became our historical consultant; he had been in Japan with the American occupation but had no previous knowledge of the footage.

Our sparse "human-effects footage" was eventually clustered near the close of our film. Its sparseness may have had some advantages. Near the beginning we placed expanses of desolation representing the central areas of the blasts, then grotesque ruins from the fringes. Their emptiness had its own eloquence. Our narration was able to add other meanings. Data from the shot lists and other sources accompanied a montage of Nagasaki remnants:

> NARRATOR: The medical college stood six hundred yards from the center; 198 faculty and students died, 128 were injured. The Nagasaki penitentiary stood three hundred yards from the center; 140 prisoners died in their cells. The Chinzei Middle School stood five hundred fifty yards from the center; most of the children died as they sat at their desks.

In another sequence we used the words of a Hiroshima girl who had survived on the edge of the blast and had later come to the United States for plastic surgery as one of the "Hiroshima maidens." Her words accompanied shots moving across wastelands and past twisted ruins.

> GIRL: I remember—I remember, a big light comes. Very strong light. I never see so strong—I do not know what is happening. My friend, she and I are always together, but I could not find her. So dark it gets, so red like fire. All is smoking dark red. I cannot see anyone. Many people run, I just follow. Pretty soon like fog, red fog, then gray—and people down all around me. Many people look so awful. Skin come off. Just awful. Makes me so scared, so afraid. I never knew such hurt on people. Not human. I think, if I am in hell, it is like this—no faces, no eyes, red and burned all things. Like women's hair, dusty and smoking with burning. Many people go into the river. I watch them. Many people are drinking water, but they fall in and die, and they float away. Voices cry, calling names. I cannot hear because so many voices cry, all calling names . . .

As the film took shape we held small previews, and we began to sense that our film could serve the purpose that, as producer, I had aimed for: to provide, without argumentation, a vivid understanding of the nature of atomic weaponry. The SECRET classification had of course impeded such understanding. We soon learned there would be further impediments.

In January 1970 we scheduled a large press preview at the Museum of Modern Art and invited the television networks. None came. But the UPI was represented, and that evening its ticker carried a report that treated the showing as a historic event. As a result, each of the networks phoned the following morning to request preview prints, and sent helmeted motorcycle couriers to the campus for them. Then came long silence. We phoned to inquire about reactions and learned that ABC and CBS had decided they were not interested. NBC said it might be interested if it could find a "news hook." We dared not speculate on what sort of event this might call for.

Then a strange sequence of media actions changed the situation. The Sunday newspaper supplement *Parade*, which generally focused on the erotic adventures of the mighty, featured an item about *Hiroshima-Nagasaki, August 1945*, calling it an important film that should be seen by the people of any nation possessing the bomb. The *Parade* item prompted *The Boston Globe*—which carried *Parade*—to phone inquiries to nuclear scientists and others, some of whom had been at our previews. On the basis of their comments, the *Globe* published a lead editorial blasting the networks for ignoring the film. The entertainment weekly *Variety*, beguiled by the *Globe*'s twitting the networks, carried a prominent box about it. This in turn led National Education Television (NET), representing public television, to begin negotiations. It arranged to telecast the film in early August, twenty-five years after the events of 1945. No sooner had this arrangement been made than NBC decided it wanted the film for its magazine series *First Tuesday*. Learning that the film was committed to NET, the NBC spokesman asked, "Couldn't you buy them out?" We declined to try.

We began to realize that the nature of atomic weapons—their implications for virtually all aspects of life on earth, including the question of its survival—was something most people preferred not to confront. The reluctance became a constant factor for us. Schools, churches, and community groups were asking for the film and arranging screenings. But expected viewers often found, at the last moment, that other commitments required their attention.

Other factors may have played a role at the commercial networks, which generally looked on documentaries as loss leaders. Documentaries not produced by the networks themselves were seldom scheduled, a policy attacked by independents as dangerously monopolistic. Yet some people at the networks were clearly intent on broadcasting *Hiroshima-Nagasaki, August 1945*, while others were averse. In the end NBC's *Today* series carried a short clip from the film, promoting the NET telecast.

We became aware of similar ambivalences in Japan. Our first inkling came at the Museum of Modern Art preview, when a representative of the Tokyo Broadcasting System (TBS), a commercial network, approached us for television rights. This puzzled us; we pointed out that a copy of the basic footage was in the hands of the Japanese government and that its announcement had mentioned plans for a television screening. The TBS representative persisted, however, and an agreement was made. Soon afterward our film appeared on TBS; a rebroadcast was scheduled almost immediately. We began to receive from Professor Sakamoto of the University of Tokyo translations of the voluminous comments from the Japanese press. Apparently our film—not yet broadcast in the United States—had "caused a sensation throughout the country," as *Mainichi Shimbun* reported. One newspaper thanked Columbia University for showing the Japanese people "what our own government tried to withhold from us." The clippings clarified for us what had happened. A government screening had taken place on NHK, the government broadcasting system, but "human-effects footage" had been removed "in deference to the relatives of victims." This had caused indignant protest—from surviving victims, relatives of victims, news media, and especially those who had been involved in the filming. Against this background TBS had negotiated for our film, and the clamor had added to the film's impact. In Hiroshima, where "viewing soared to four times the normal rate," the newspaper *Chugoku Shimbun* reported on the viewing of a special group.

An especially gratifying response came from Akira Iwasaki, who after a lapse of almost twenty-five years had seen his footage on television. He wrote us long letters expressing his appreciation of our handling of the footage. He showed no resentment over the absence of credit to him. He published a long review in a leading Japanese magazine, describing his reactions:

I was lost in thought for a long time, deeply moved by this film. . . . I was the producer of the original long film which offered the basic material for this short film. That is, I knew every cut of it . . . yet I was speechless. . . . It was not the kind of film the Japanese thought the Americans would produce. The film is an appeal or warning from man to man for peaceful reflection—to prevent the use of the bomb ever again. I like this narration, in which the emotion is well controlled and the voice is never raised. . . . That made me cry. In this part, the producers were no longer Americans. Their feelings are completely identical to our feelings.

From clippings and letters the history of the footage began to emerge. After the two bombs had fallen, the Japanese Education Ministry had commissioned Nippon Eiga Sha to document the effects of the mysterious new weapon. Because of the chaos and the breakdown of transportation, it had taken the film crews some days to reach the two bombed cities, but they were at work when the American occupation forces arrived. What happened then was described in one of Iwasaki's letters to us: "In the middle of the shooting, one of my cameramen was arrested by Nagasaki and American military police. . . . I was summoned to GHQ and told to discontinue the shooting." Filming was halted but, according to Iwasaki, he "made arguments" wherever he could. "Then," he wrote, "came the group of the Strategic Bombing Survey from Washington and they wanted to have a film of Hiroshima and Nagasaki. Therefore the U.S. Army wanted to utilize my film . . . and changed its mind. Now they allowed—or, better—ordered me to continue. . . ." Thus, under close U.S. supervision, additional hours of footage were shot during the following weeks and its arrangement into sequences was begun. When the assemblage had achieved a length of some two hours and forty minutes the saga entered a new phase. One day "the film negative, positive, and every piece of short end were confiscated and carried away by the U.S. Army to Washington." Classified SECRET, the material disappeared from view for almost a quarter of a century. Few knew of its existence.

On August 3, 1970, *Hiroshima-Nagasaki, August 1945* received its American television premiere on NET, and won for the noncommercial system one of its largest audiences to date. "HIROSHIMA GETS NUMBERS," *Variety* reported. NET's Tampa outlet carried the film on a delayed basis via tape after deleting "human-effects footage." Thus the ambivalence continued. But NET's decision to show the film was widely acclaimed.

During the following years many libraries and community groups acquired prints and held showings. But in the mid-1970's Columbia University Press decided to discontinue its film activities, and distribution of *Hiroshima-Nagasaki, August 1945* lapsed for several years. Then the recent upsurge of talk about a "winnable" nuclear war stirred new interest in our film. The film was taken over by International Film Seminars, organizers of the Flaherty Seminars and custodians of *Nanook of the North* and other Flaherty classics. It assigned distribution rights to the Museum of Modern Art. Intensive users of the film now included Physicians for Social Responsibility, and a new review in the *Bulletin of the Atomic Scientists* called it "required viewing for all who are concerned about the survivability of mankind." Demand for the film began a sudden and dramatic escalation. At the Museum of Modern Art it became the number one film in both sales and rentals.

Because of the renewed and mounting interest in the film, I have placed in the Special Collections division of the Columbia University Libraries the complete file of letters, memoranda, and other documents relating to the evolution of *Hiroshima-Nagasaki, August 1945*—some three hundred items in all. All documents cited in this article are included. Copies of the entire file have also been placed in the study section of the Museum of Modern Art; in the film division of the Library of Congress; and in the Imperial War Museum, London.

Since the completion of our film I have visited Japan twice, had long talks with Akira Iwasaki, met one of the cameramen in his 1945 unit, and visited the generously helpful Professor Sakamoto. I continued to correspond with Iwasaki until his death in September 1981. To prints of *Hiroshima-Nagasaki, August 1945* now distributed by the Museum of Modern Art an afterword has been added: "The original Japanese footage was shot by Nippon Eiga Sha under Akira Iwasaki."

11

The Zig-Zag Career of Radio Luxembourg

RADIO LUXEMBOURG was, from the start, an odd phenomenon. Spawned by one of Europe's mini-countries, it had one of the continent's most potent transmitters, able to penetrate to its outer reaches. With 150,000 watts, it had three times the power of America's strongest domestic stations, at this time limited to 50,000 watts. During the 1930s much of the Radio Luxembourg programming was beamed to Britain, in English, in the interests of commercial sponsors, who were mainly American. British broadcasting was still entirely non-commercial. American manufacturers of toiletries, household products and packaged foods, eager to duplicate their American radio-advertising successes in Europe, especially in the British Isles, found Radio Luxembourg ready to serve their desires. The station had some competition in this from Radio Normandy, but Radio Luxembourg was far more powerful and successful, and had built a large British following with programming that included American jazz and soap operas.[1]

In the spring of 1940 the German armies, sweeping westward, took possession of the station and proceeded to use it for their own proselytizing. It was clearly of immense propaganda value. In 1944, as the Allied troops drove in the opposite direction, Allied psychological warfare units were following closely behind, seizing any radio facilities they found available. They especially had their eyes on Radio Luxembourg, but scarcely expected to find it in usable shape.

At the station the retreating Germans set dynamite charges but—inexplicably—failed to detonate them. It is said that the Radio Luxembourg head engineer, who had served the Germans throughout their occupation and use of the station, encouraged them at the time of their departure to shoot holes through the transmitter tubes. Perhaps his idea was to divert them from more catastrophic destruction. When the Americans arrived, he dug up from the garden a complete duplicate set of tubes he had buried four years earlier for such a day.[2] This enabled the station to resume broadcasting twelve days after the Allied entry into Luxembourg. On September 22, 1944, "Radio Free Luxembourg" went on the air as the special instrument of the psychological warfare unit of the 12th U.S. Army group. Miraculously, a large collection of undamaged Guy Lombardo, Benny Goodman, Dorsey Brothers, Glenn Miller and other phonograph records—mostly from prewar days but used by the Germans for their own radio blandishments—was found available, and was put to work for Allied purposes.[3]

Radio Luxembourg now launched a variety of programming. The activities came under the executive supervision—generally exercised from Paris—of such luminaries as William S. Paley and Davidson Taylor of CBS and Allied counterparts, all seasoned radio veterans who had gone into uniform for psychological warfare duty. At the station the administrator was William Harlan Hale. But the propaganda strategy was the work of the remarkable Hans Habe.

Hans Habe, originally named Janos Bekessy, was born in Hungary in 1911. A prominent journalist and newspaper editor in prewar Vienna, he claimed credit for the discovery that Hitler's name was Schicklgruber. Bekessy fled Austria in 1939, enlisted in the French army, was captured by the Germans, managed a romantic escape through concealment in a brothel, made his way to Vichy and thence to the United States, and then enlisted in the American army. After special training he performed psychological warfare services in North Africa and Italy. Now, with the advance into Germany, he became the key strategist at Radio Luxembourg. Because the name Bekessy was on a Nazi execution list, he now lived under the name Hans Habe. At Radio Luxembourg he directed both its "white" and "black"—acknowledged and unacknowledged—broadcasting activities.[4]

During daytime and evening hours, with its full power and established frequency, Radio Free Luxembourg addressed Germans in the German language, as an avowedly American voice. It offered frequent news programs called *Frontpost*, a title also used on millions of leaflets showered on Germany during the advance.

A potent *Frontpost* feature was a daily segment called *Briefe die Sie nicht erreichten (Letters That Didn't Reach You)*. It consisted of excerpts from the huge quantities of undelivered German mail seized during the Allied drive through France. The selections were very simply read aloud by a Luxembourg girl with a warm, appealing voice. The personal nature of this material was probably a powerful factor in winning attention for the station. American staff members were among those who found the letters deeply moving, mirroring as they did the total disruption of lives everywhere.[5]

Another feature, designed as a spur to desertions from the German forces, was a carefully selected procession of prisoners brought to the Radio Free Luxembourg microphones, who said in effect—in one way or another—"Hello Mother! I'm safe! I'm a prisoner of the Americans!" The selection of prisoners for these on-the-air appearances was supervised with care by Habe.

There were also grimmer features. Two Germans in civilian clothes had been captured nearby on an espionage mission. Radio Free Luxembourg broadcast their trial, and then interviewed the convicted prisoners en route to the prison courtyard. Asked if they realized that the penalty for what they had done was death, the prisoners said no, their officers had not told them that. Shortly afterwards the radio audience was allowed to hear the click of the rifle bolts, the shouted commands, the volley, and the echo of the rifle fire. *Yank*, the serviceman's magazine, thought this was probably the first on-the-air execution.[6]

In contrast, the station also made successful use of humor. This revolved around a figure presented as "Corporal Tom Jones," said to come from Green Bay, Wisconsin. He was actually a synthetic figure, whose evolution was again masterminded by Hans Habe.

Though *Yank* referred to Corporal Tom Jones as "a sort of Central European Bob Hope," Jones was never brash. Rather, he spoke in a guileless, unassuming manner, which soon won him a flood of mash notes.

The voice was that of Richard Hanser, former city editor of the newspaper *PM*. He had never been to Green Bay, Wisconsin; he had been born in Buffalo, New York, in 1909. It was Hans Habe who decided that Tom Jones should be from Green Bay; it sounded so American to him. Hanser had once studied for the ministry at Concordia Lutheran Institute of Bronxville, New York, which required every student to learn enough German to deliver a sermon in that language. Thus Hanser had some fluency in German, along with a quaint accent that Germans tended to find utterly charming, and which won him the role of Jones. Hanser, a civilian on the OWI staff, was then put into uniform and assigned to the 12th U.S. Army group with "assimilated" rank as a major, though his on-the-air role was that of a corporal.

The "Corporal Tom Jones" segments, inserted each evening into the 8:00–8:15 *Frontpost* program, were never argumentative or hortatory. They included matters seemingly unrelated to the war—a key part of Habe's strategy. Jones would reminisce about things he did as a boy in his spare time in Green Bay. The aim was to suggest an extreme personal freedom, devoid of obligatory youth groups. It probably conveyed a Huck Finn aura, of much appeal in the turmoil of war.

One element in the humor did relate to the war. Corporal Jones would relay underground jokes he said he had heard from German prisoners—anti-Nazi jokes, known as *Flusterwitze,* or whisper-jokes. Here was forbidden matter suddenly emerging on the public airwaves. Hundreds of such jokes were collected via interviews with prisoners, and they became a regular "Corporal Tom Jones" sign-off feature and a smash hit. Some were *Galgenhumor,* gallows humor, but Jones relayed them ingenuously, as though not quite understanding their devastating significance. Hanser, whom I interviewed at length, remembered the following:

> They used to say, "No enemy aircraft over the Reich!" They still say it, but differently. Now they say, "No Reich under the enemy aircraft!"
>
> In the old days, it used to be that you'd go to the railway station, and the train was gone. Now you go for a train, and the station is gone.
>
> A man told a Gestapo agent, "I'd rather work for the Nazis than anyone else!" The pleased Gestapo agent asked, "What sort of work do you do?" "I'm a gravedigger."[7]

Word of "Corporal Tom Jones's" fame eventually spread to Green Bay, his alleged hometown. As a result, the Associated Press received a request from a Green Bay newspaper editor for information about its famous son. The A.P. actually dispatched someone to Luxembourg to interview Jones, but the Corporal's true identity was kept secret.[8]

The programs mentioned so far were part of Radio Luxembourg's daytime and evening offerings as an acknowledged American voice, heard over radio Luxembourg's regular place on the dial, with its full available power. But the psychological warfare group also used the transmitter for an entirely different activity, which occupied the middle of the night, 2:00–6:00 A.M.

Using lower power, 30,000 watts, the station now purported to be an underground German station operating behind German lines. It used a different frequency—1212 kilocycles—and called itself Twelve Twelve. It went on the air with: "Hello, this is Twelve Twelve calling." It was not overtly anti-Nazi but suggested that the German authorities were fallible and making mistakes. On every program Twelve Twelve carried detailed, scrupulously accurate reports about the military situation within Germany. Its task, at this stage, was to establish total credibility and trust. Only a few German voices, of a regional quality to suggest a location in the Rhine valley, were used on Twelve Twelve. The idea was to convey the image of a compact underground group.

Much of its strategy had been planned in advance. Music was never used—only talk. The Twelve Twelve team was made to live in isolation, to avoid any hint of interaction with other Radio Luxembourg programming. The group was housed in a fine villa in Luxembourg's Rue Brasseur, once the property of a German coal mine manager. Military police guarded the premises day and night.[9]

That the group's programs were soon winning trust was reflected in the fact that prisoners, when interrogated about the situation within Germany, began to quote Twelve Twelve. But the winning of trust was only the first step. The trust had a purpose: it was a weapon, potentially devastating. During the Moselle assault and breakthrough by Allied troops, Twelve Twelve suddenly began to create chaos with rampant disinformation. Among other bulletins, it reported Allied tanks near Nuremberg and Friedrichshafen, causing panic in those cities. This confusion was its ultimate task. Immediately afterwards, its job done, Twelve Twelve vanished as abruptly as it had appeared. It had been on the air just 127 nights.[10]

Hans Habe, chief Luxembourg broadcasting strategist during this period, was awarded the Bronze Star with Oak Leaf Cluster, and the Luxembourg Croix de Guerre. Under the Allied occupation of Germany he was for a time in charge of all German newspapers, but seems to have had a falling out with the Occupation and resumed his peripatetic, often flamboyant career. He wrote a number of novels based on his war exploits, some of which were translated into

English—including *Walk in Darkness, Off Limits,* and *The Mission.*
He had brief Hollywood sojourns and wrote an autobiography, *All My Sins.* His five marriages in five different countries included one to the daughter of the legendarily wealthy Marjorie Merryweather Post, Post Toasties heiress who had married Ambassador Joseph E. Davies. Habe eventually settled in Switzerland.

Richard Hanser served a postwar stint as writer of RKO-Pathe on the *This is America* series of film shorts, then had a distinguished television career as chief writer for NBC's Project Twenty documentaries, and coauthor with Henry Salomon of the *Victory at Sea* series. He published books that included *Putsch! how Hitler made revolution* and *A Noble Treason: the revolt of the Munich students against Hitler.* He was the translator of *Walk in Darkness,* one of the novels of his former mentor Hans Habe.

Of all Radio Luxembourg's activities under the psychological warfare group, the Twelve Twelve caper was perhaps the most innovative, and an extraordinary success. I remember being dazzled by what I heard and read about it. At a time when people were just beginning to talk about "black radio," this was the most telling example of what it could do. It also appears to have been the one psychological warfare maneuver that influenced postwar years.

There seem by now to have been countless "black radio" ventures by many countries in many places.[11] About most of these it is almost impossible to gather reliable details, and a substantial overview of the topic may never be possible. But about one such venture we know a great deal, mainly because it—and the military venture it supported—ended in failure and detailed exposure. This "black radio" venture was a close copy of Twelve Twelve. I am referring to Radio Swan, the mysterious station established in connection with the Bay of Pigs invasion of Cuba.

The similarities were numerous. The station purported to be the activity of a dissident underground group—in this case, at odds with the Castro regime. The station was actually a covert U.S. venture—in this case, financed, planned and controlled by the CIA, though featuring Cuban voices.

The military offensive, in this case, was an invasion to be launched from Nicaragua, for which purpose the CIA had assembled nine ships, thirty-seven planes, tanks, bombs, rockets and all sorts of ammunition, and trained a Cuban assault force at a secret camp in the mountains of Guatemala.[12] The CIA was predicting—in intra-administration discussions—that the landing of this force would cause a quarter of the Cuban population to rise in support, and overthrow Castro.[13]

Months before the invasion date, the mysterious radio station began its work. It never mentioned the invasion preparations; it seemed oblivious to any such activity. Its broadcasts spoke of problems and dissatisfactions within Cuba, blunders of the Castro regime, and expectations of a spontaneous uprising in the foreseeable future.

The station operated from barren Swan Island—actually, two tiny islands several hundred miles south of the western tip of Cuba. Again, the location made a hermetic isolation possible. The broadcasts gave the impression of a compact group of recent émigrés, in touch with fellow dissidents in Cuba.

Once more, the first task was to establish credibility. Radio Swan did so, over many months, by accurate details of life in Cuba. Actually, some of the programs were pre-recorded in the United States; a CIA plane is said to have come once a week from the United States, with the recordings to be used.[14]

Operating with a power of 50,000 watts, the station could be heard in parts of the United States. Journalists began to consider it a reliable source of information about events in Cuba, and to quote its bulletins. Again, the trust was a weapon.

When the assault from Nicaragua finally began, the station's task was to foment an uprising and to sow confusion. It broadcast sabotage instructions. And, with staccato proclamations and jubilant reportage, it broadcast bulletins prepared in advance to fit the CIA scenario of a spontaneous uprising. Similar bulletins were issued in New York in the name of a Cuban Revolutionary Council—bulletins likewise planted by the CIA, which had formed the so-called Council. The fact that its bulletins dovetailed with Radio Swan bulletins seemed to authenticate both. The substance of the bulletins was that the Cuban people were rising in revolt; that Castro's air force had defected; that defecting pilots had bombed and destroyed their own air bases; that one of the defecting pilots, in a bullet-riddled plane, was heading for Florida; that he had reached Florida; that the Castro regime was in utter panic; and that "freedom" was imminent.[15]

As we now know, none of the events quite followed this scenario. The invasion collapsed quickly. The people did not rise.

To be sure, a Cuban pilot with a bullet-punctured plane did reach Florida; photographs of the plane and bullet holes appeared in the American press and on American television. But this plane, falsely marked to appear to be a Castro plane, had flown direct from Nicaragua; its markings and bullet holes were CIA fabrications, as was the whole episode.

During the following months the failure of the invasion was discussed in various forums. A four-man government committee of inquiry ascribed the failure to a "shortage of ammunition." Two of the members of this committee had been leaders in planning the operation; one of them was Allen Dulles. This committee gave little attention to the non-military aspects of the venture. But the role of Radio Swan was later exhaustively reviewed by investigating journalists via interviews with government officials and ex-officials, and with the Cuban exiles who had been drawn into various phases of the operation. Some comment on the Radio Swan activity seems in order here.

Having been dazzled by the Twelve Twelve caper of World War II, what is one to think of this later venture, so similar in technique? It should be noted, of course, that the United States was in a declared war with Germany, not with Cuba. Allen Dulles, master planner of the Bay of Pigs operation, had phraseology to circumvent this problem. In *The Craft of Intelligence*, written as a sort of justification of his career, he wrote that the United States was not "really" at peace, since communism had "declared its own war on our system of government and life." He therefore saw the rules of war as applicable.[16] This formulation apparently seemed convincing to many, and may satisfy some even now.

The carrying over of "black radio" into peacetime clearly raises legal, ethical, and moral questions beyond the scope of this discussion. But its use is often defended as a practical necessity in a turbulent age—defended in the name of realism. So perhaps, in discussing Radio Swan, we should at least assess it in terms of *Realpolitik*.

At the hour of crisis Radio Swan, like Twelve Twelve, succeeded in creating widespread confusion—though less within Cuba than elsewhere. In the case of the Bay of Pigs venture, the tissue of disinformation succeeded mainly in deceiving American newspapers and broadcasting systems, and through them the American people. And the deception reached further.

Tragically, there came a moment when Adlai Stevenson, America's much-admired spokesman at the United Nations, who had not been taken into confidence about the CIA caper but thought he had correct information, stood before the General Assembly and denied any U.S. involvement in the events in Cuba. It was simply, he said, a spontaneous Cuban uprising. As evidence he cited a defecting Castro pilot who had escaped to safety in Florida in a bullet-riddled plane. In proof, Stevenson held up a photo for the General Assembly, the television cameras, and all the world to see. Within days he learned that his own statements had been false, and that he had been duped by his own government. It was a devastating moment in Stevenson's career.[17]

It was also devastating for the United States. The credibility of its official utterances had been thrown into question, at a long-range cost not easy to assess. Clearly trickery in the use of media is a two-edged weapon—especially in a time that must technically be described as peace.

World War II, besides being a declared war, was a period of extraordinary consensus. Few wars in our history seem to have been so broadly supported. Hitler had helped to make this possible—had helped to make it, for many, a kind of holy war. Perhaps, in a way, this has proved a trap. We came to take it fully for granted that we represented truth and justice—that we were the ones on the white horses—and we carried into later years the feeling we could do no wrong and that whatever we did, by whatever means, was automatically in the interest of freedom, democracy, and peace. That was perhaps our most dangerous heritage from World War II.

Notes

1. B. Paulu, *British Broadcasting: radio and television in the United Kingdom* (Minneapolis: 1956), pp. 26–31, 360–61.

2. *Yank*, May 11, 1945. Also D. Taylor, in Columbia University Oral History interview (New York: 1956), p. 43.

3. R. Hanser, in Columbia University Oral History interview (New York: 1967), pp. 5–6.

4. H. Habe, *All My Sins: an autobiography* (London: 1957), pp. 340–50.

5. Hanser, *op. cit.*, pp.7–14.

6. *Yank*, May 11, 1945.

7. Broadcast on *Frontpost*, Dec. 11, 1944; Apr. 6, 15, 1945.

8. Hanser, *op. cit.*, pp. 7–14.

9. Habe, *op. cit.*, p. 347.

10. *Publicity and Psychological Warfare, 12th Army Group: History, January 1943–August 1945* (ETO, undated), pp. 197–200.

11. D. Wise, and T. Ross, *The Invisible Government* (New York: 1964), pp. 313–37. Also T. C. Sorenson, *The Word War: The Story of American Propaganda* (New York: 1968), pp. 11–12.

12. Invasion details based on H. Johnson, with M. Artime, and others, *The Bay of Pigs: The Leaders' Story of Brigade 2506* (New York: 1964); other sources as noted.

13. A. M. Schlesinger, Jr., *A Thousand Days: John F. Kennedy in the White House* (Boston: 1965), p. 247.

14. Wise and Ross, *op. cit.*, pp. 328–37.

15. *Ibid.*, pp. 29–72.

16. A. Dulles, *The Craft of Intelligence* (New York: 1963), p. 54, pp. 230–31.

17. D. Wise, *The Politics of Lying: Government Deception, Secrecy, and Power* (New York: 1973), pp. 53–54.

12

Historical Survey of Communications Breakthroughs

EUPHORIC PREDICTIONS greeted the advent of Morse's telegraph and the communication wonders that followed it—telephone, wireless, radio, television, and others. Each was seen to have special significance for a democratic society: each seemed to promise wider dissemination of information and ideas. It can be argued that this has happened, as predicted. But other results, in a contrary direction, were not so readily foreseen. Each new medium offered new possibilities for the centralization of influence and control, and introduced new monopoly possibilities. This essay examines the conflicting tendencies—inherent, to a large extent, in the technologies themselves—and may help in assessing the impact of new technological breakthroughs.

The invention of the telegraph made it possible for the first time to link distant areas by wire. The telegraph industry was founded by both large and small entrepreneurs, but the larger tended to absorb or otherwise eliminate the smaller. Soon after the Civil War the Western Union Telegraph Co. achieved a dominant position—it became virtually a monopoly. By 1873 its wires reached into thirty-seven states and nine territories and constituted the only nationwide web.

It is difficult to reconstruct the impact of the Western Union monopoly, but historians of the telegraph indicated that it yielded extraordinary wealth and power. In 1875, Representative Charles A. Sumner of California charged that news of sudden changes in market prices was repeatedly withheld from San Francisco until insiders had made large profits. Control of the flow of information apparently provided even more advantages than the profits made from the message business, which, monopoly-priced, was a bonanza in itself. Proposals to end the monopoly power by creating a government telegraph service linking U.S. post offices by an alternative web of wires—an idea that took hold in Europe—were repeatedly introduced in Congress in the decades after the Civil War, but Western Union always mustered crushing opposition. It worked in close alliance with the old Associated Press, which relied on Western Union wires. Newspapers aspiring to effective national or international coverage were totally dependent on these two monopolistic allies. It is said that newspapers backing postal telegraph proposals found their rates raised or service canceled. Publishers, editors, and reporters got accustomed to the idea that discussing postal ("socialistic") telegraphy was taboo.

Western Union had other persuasive pressures. Friendly legislators received "franks"—vouchers providing free telegraph privileges—in apparently unlimited quantities. Alvin Harlow quoted a letter to a New York politician from a Western Union official:

> Dear Mr.:
>   I enclose another book of franks, of which I have extended the limits to cover all Western Union lines. I hope they will help you make a good nomination. Please use them freely on political messages, and telegraph me when you want a fresh supply.[1]

Politicians of both major parties shared in these benefits. In 1873, Western Union's president, William Orton, told his board of directors that the company's operations were subject to government action at various levels, and that the franks had saved revenue "many times the money value of the free service."[2] The power exercised by Western Union seems to have been used ruthlessly when it came under the control of Jay Gould. His hold over railroads, telegraph, newspapers, and politicians aroused exceptional fury, expressed in a song of the 1880s:

> We'll hang Jay Gould from a sour apple tree
> And bring to grief the plotters of a base monopoly.[3]

The influence of the communications monopoly over the political situation of the era may well have been considerable. The monopoly was eventually ended by Alexander Graham Bell's telephone, which generated its own web of wires. Western Union tried to forestall this competition with patent litigation against the infant Bell company.

In 1879 Bell's successful emergence from this onslaught—contrary to most expectations—caused the company's stock to leap within weeks from $50 to $995 a share. A few years later the incorporation certificate of the American Telephone and Telegraph Company (AT&T) dazzlingly foreshadowed the future in store for the new medium. Dated 1885, it empowered the company to link every city, town, and place in the United States, Canada, and Mexico "with each and every other city, town or place in said states and countries, and also by cable and other appropriate means with the rest of the known world, as may hereafter become necessary or desirable in conducting the business of this association."[4]

By 1909, AT&T was so wealthy that it bought control of Western Union with a $30 million check, and its president, Theodore B. Vail, also became president of Western Union. But by this time, antimonopoly sentiments had made headway, and the move was prohibited by government action. By this time also, the invention of the wireless, soon followed by radio, had created additional opportunities for the dissemination of information and ideas. The erosion of monopoly control had even permitted another telegraph company to come into existence, the Postal Telegraph Company. This private corporation, not connected with the postal system, adopted its name because of its antimonopoly ring. The Postal Telegraph Company later evolved into the powerful International Telephone & Telegraph Corporation (ITT). The monopoly's collapse also saw the rise of United Press International as a news-distribution agency offering competition to the Associated Press. All these developments seemed to rule out a return to the monopolistic nightmare of the Western Union heyday.

Yet the mix of contemporary communications technologies includes one element that, in the light of the history here recounted, deserves more attention than it has received. One of the most extraordinary of the new developments is optical fiber. AT&T, a leading pioneer in this development, refers to it as "lightwave communication," because it is based on the flow of laser beams through glass fibers. A glass thread the thickness of a human hair far exceeds the more bulky and expensive coaxial cable in its message-carrying capacity. A thin, compact cord of such fibers can thus serve a home, office, or other location with telephone, television, computer, and numerous other services, some involving two-way communication.

The single link could thus bring to a home "communication center" not only all the entertainment and news services provided by present television and cable systems but also the means for such added features as sight-and-sound telephone, television conferences (with documents provided via printout), television shopping, voting, banking, mail delivery, and television use of film archives, museums, and educational offerings. The possibilities involved in this scenario— the technical feasibility of which is no longer in doubt —are so overwhelming that little attention has been paid to the fact that all these innovations could enter the home, office, or other location through a single fiber connection. Would this create an extraordinary new monopolistic possibility? To be sure, the scenario envisages a multiplicity of choices for the citizen, but it is not limitless. At some stage a preliminary process of selection would be involved—not by the home but by a "lightwave communication" company. In its possibilities for control, would it revive the possibility of a monopoly like the one Western Union enjoyed? This question must be considered in combination with similar ambiguities involved in other new developments.

LICENSED COMMUNICATION

The regulatory control system set up for radio and television by the Radio Act of 1927 (PL-632) and the Communications Act of 1934 (PL-416) was essentially a licensing system, requiring government permission to communicate through these media. The technical nature of the media seemed to make such an arrangement necessary, if spectrum chaos was to be avoided. Yet the system would surely have disturbed the Founding Fathers, to whom licensed communication was anathema.

It was by licensing systems that rulers of Europe sought to control the dissemination of heresies during the centuries following the invention of the printing press. Under Henry VIII the operation of a printing press required royal permission; licensed printers, blessed by royal privilege, became gatekeepers of the society. John Milton wrote his *Areopagitica*, a protest pamphlet issued without the seal of approval, against such systems. This pamphlet denounced rulers for stifling "the winds of doctrine" with licensing requirements. He helped to make this a cause célèbre for generations of thinkers, including the Founding Fathers of the United States. The term "freedom of the press" in the Bill of Rights meant precisely freedom from licensing. America's founders were determined that in the new nation no one would need government permission to communicate with the public.

But the radio and television age did launch such a system of licensing. Some lawmakers felt troubled over this, so the new legislation provided that the regulatory commission—first the Federal Radio Commission (FRC), later the Federal Communications Commission (FCC)—must not act as censor. Its power was to lie in the right to renew or not renew a license at periodic intervals. The ban on ad hoc censorship strengthened the position of licensees vis-à-vis the commissions but did not touch the basic problem. Licensed broadcasters, like licensed printers of past centuries, had become increasingly powerful gatekeepers as the regulatory commissions tended to fall under industry control and became reluctant to regulate. With television becoming the chief source of information and ideas about world events for most Americans, the gatekeeper role has assumed central political significance. For groups and individuals, access to the electorate has become dependent on access to television. The election process has come to hinge on it.

It is widely argued, with some plausibility, that the array of new technologies has eliminated the problem. Cable television's multiplicity of channels has supposedly ended channel scarcity and made deregulation a safe policy, so that the broadcast media can now be left to market forces. This argument ignores the fact that the real issue has not been a scarcity of channels but the need for a government license to communicate. Cable systems are also licensed systems. Each is a local monopoly requiring a local franchise, in which acknowledged or unacknowledged political considerations can again play a part. Cable systems may revive some of the power of local political bosses, which network broadcasting is said to have severely weakened. In any case, these systems are clearly creating a new gatekeeping echelon.

The satellites by which cable systems are fed and linked are likewise government-licensed entities and create still another such echelon. These, like the cable systems, are high-technology and capital-intensive developments. With deregulation already proceeding, both satellite and cable systems are falling increasingly under the control of companies long associated with the media monopolies—AT&T, Western Union, ITT, General Electric, Westinghouse, Warner Communications, and RCA. To be sure, the central issue is access rather than ownership. This matter should therefore be examined in the context of still another area of ambiguity and conflict—the terms and costs of access.

SELLING AIR TIME

When in 1922 AT&T pioneered the selling of air time in the way newspaper space was sold, the idea was prominently criticized as an offensive and unseemly intrusion of advertising into the home. A long-range political impact was foreseen by few.

Programming of every sort involves political implications; it reflects and in turn reinforces prevailing cultural assumptions. The direct and indirect influence of advertisers over sponsored programming, a large subject in itself, is too complex for detailed consideration here. But politicians and political scientists have generally been most concerned about the politician's access to the broadcast media as a means of access to the electorate.

American commercial broadcasters early established a close relationship with incumbent legislators, not unlike the relationship built around the "franks" of the Western Union monopoly. Legislators have regularly received free time to "report to their constituents"—in effect, a boost toward reelection—and this has in turn given broadcasting executives ready access to legislators. This close alliance has resembled the Western Union–Associated Press alliance of earlier days. But the free time has applied only to non-campaign periods. During election campaigns, when time-seekers are often numerous and in many cases unlikely to be successful, broadcasting time has generally been available only on a for-sale basis. This system has prevailed in the United States. But in most other Western democracies, time for important campaigns has been available free, by law, with allocations made on a mathematical basis—that is, in proportion to party enrollment, to representation in a legislature, or to votes in a previous election. Most European countries have outlawed the sale of time for political messages.

Even though the time-sale method has prevailed in the United States, broadcasters have never been eager to sell time for political appeals, especially when it meant preempting time occupied by popular and profitable entertainment. Political programs generally lose part of the audience to rival stations. Equal-time requirements have resulted in lower revenue for the stations, and broadcasters have accordingly sought to discourage political time purchases. Forbidden to charge higher than commercial rates (some had, for a time, levied higher charges), they introduced other obstacles. In the Standard Rate and Data volumes of the 1930s, a special rule appears for political broadcasts—cash in advance. Presumably, it was difficult to collect from an unsuccessful candidate and perhaps even more difficult to collect from a successful candidate. Candidates often had to arrive at stations with bundles of cash in envelopes.

Even with cash in advance, campaigning candidates have not been warmly welcomed. With time often on a sold-out basis and with prices rising, candidates have gradually been squeezed into making campaign appeals in thirty- and sixty-second advertising slots. The use of longer periods has virtually vanished. The shift has made electioneering increasingly simplistic, while giving the field of politics an air of hucksterism. But a more dangerous result may be the growing role of finance in the process.

The price of a thirty-second network slot, negotiated on a slot-by-slot basis, may vary from a few hundred dollars to more than $100,000, depending on the supposed size and nature of the audience of the surrounding programming. Local rates may likewise vary widely. Commercial sponsors will pay more for larger audiences and still more for spots that reach precisely their target sales audiences. Targets may be defined demographically—for example, "women 25 through 34 years old." Sponsors try to match program audience to product market and plot their appeals accordingly. The system pushes networks and stations into eliminating or sidetracking programs that do not yield high-value advertising slots. The low status of world and national news in network planning—twenty-three early-evening minutes preliminary to the main concerns of the evening—reflects the sales-dominated atmosphere. Politicians, hoping to reach an audience, thus find themselves caught in an expensive game of social engineering. Each segment of the audience seems to have its special price tag. Inevitably, politicians turn to advertising agencies to guide them through the time-buying maze and turn to pollsters, advertising writers, sophisticated producers, and special-effects virtuosos to develop their appeal strategies. The cost mounts accordingly.

The textbook view of the evolution of American democracy is that it began with government by the few—male, white property-owners who constituted most of the voting population—but that the base has steadily expanded. In the early decades of the Republic, propertyless men won the vote and helped to create the Jacksonian era. Legislation after the Civil War enfranchised blacks, although enforcing the process was long blocked by such regional devices as the poll tax, literacy tests, and the white primary—key obstacles eventually eliminated by litigation. Women were enfranchised following World War I, and subsequent wars led to a lowering of the voting age. Extending the franchise appears to mean a broadening of the democratic base. But it can be argued that the broadcast era has reversed democratization by creating effective financial barriers to political action.

Running for major office with a television campaign requires access to staggering funds. A candidate not independently wealthy must get funds from others—individual donors or, increasingly, political action committees (PACs). PACs acquired special importance through the Federal Election Campaign Act of 1974, which was offered as a "reform" act. This law made it illegal for a candidate to receive more than $1,000 from any one donor. But there has been no limit on gifts to PACs, which have also been relatively unconstrained on how they spend money. The law appeared to have only minor effects on the 1976 elections, but in 1980 it clearly played a major role. PACs were organized by many kinds of groups. Business-related PACs, with unprecedented war chests solicited from employees, stockholders, clients, and others, proved especially influential. PACs mounted their own campaigns while also making campaign donations to candidates—donations that went primarily into television and radio drives. A congressional candidate regarded as pivotal might receive $100,000 or more in gifts from PACs.

To what extent has the value of the vote been eroded by the quest for donations and the commitments, spoken and unspoken, involved in the process? Money has always played a part in political campaigns, but it has recently acquired a decisive role, narrowing voter choices to those backed by the top economic groups. A constriction rather than a diffusion of power seems to be involved. Voter apathy, as reflected in lower voter turnout, may well be related to a pervasive sense of ineffectuality. But true believers in the new media feel that these technologies will, in the long run, bring wider and more intense citizen involvement. To support this argument, they cite a number of developments that are felt to offer the average citizen a more active media role.

Public Access

One of these developments is the public-access channel. At one time the FCC required major cable systems to include a provision for such channels that would give the average citizen free access on a first-come basis. A court decision invalidated the FCC requirement, but many cities continue to include such a provision in local franchises. Results of public access have been mixed. Use of these channels has at times been exhibitionistic, drab, and trivial. Catering to diverse interests, the channels have seldom won a steady audience, and their significance is thereby diminished. The result is a sort of electronic Hyde Park corner, a place to express views on any subject to little effect. If in some locations the channels have played a meaningful role, it is partly because participating groups have used for their programming another new development, known as video—the use of videotape as an independent medium of expression. Low-cost and extraordinarily flexible, video may well prove a surprise factor in media competition.

Videotape entered the media industry in a quite different role. Videotape recorders, introduced in the 1950s with prices of at least $40,000, offered networks an improved means for recording and re-broadcasting live television programs. The videotape recorder promptly replaced the unsatisfactory kinescope, a film made by focusing a camera on a television tube during a performance. As videotape recorders fell sharply in price and became more convenient with the advent of cassettes, recorders began to be used in schools and homes for keeping copies of programs. Finally, with the introduction of videotape cameras and editing equipment, both increasingly compact, video became an instrument of production with unique characteristics. As equipment prices continued to drop these characteristics appeared to offer revolutionary possibilities.

Video's images can be astonishing. Unlike film images, they require no developing and no laboratories. Production does not call for special lighting or for a studio. An individual can be a production unit. Reusable and low-cost, tape can be expended almost as freely as an author uses paper. The camera, comparable in cost to a good typewriter, is easy to operate. Shots can be evaluated instantly and reshot if unsatisfactory. These characteristics give a new ease and spontaneity to the production process. Tape-editing equipment brings complex special effects within reach of individuals.

The advent of small computers has further expanded video's possibilities. Suddenly all sorts of people—individually or in schools, churches, interest groups, businesses—could enter video production. Such individuals or groups made documentaries, animated films, satires, dramas, and political arguments. Television screens already in place in homes and other locations were their ultimate link with audiences. The audience could be reached through various routes through the networks, by cable systems, or by satellites. But all of the licensed distribution systems and their gatekeepers could also be bypassed. The cassette is itself a delivery system. The compact half-inch, paperback-sized cassette can be distributed like a book and marketed by mail or through retail outlets. Easy to duplicate, cassettes lend themselves to small or large editions.

Citizen groups—political, ethnic, and others—have begun using video with dramatic results to document social problems. Antinuclear and environmental groups have been especially prominent. In some cases they have found networks or cable systems ready to carry their material. In others they have distributed cassettes to local groups for community meetings or local telecasts. These possibilities may enable video to become an important dissent medium with a role analogous to that long played by such periodicals as *The Nation* and *The New Republic*. Effective as a springboard for group discussion, video may bring a new dimension of its own to the dissent role. Of similar importance is its possible capacity to decentralize the production of images and sounds and to wrest control from major production centers. The medium has distribution problems. There are also problems relating to competing products with incompatible standards. Once such problems are resolved, however, the medium may well give an effective voice to groups that were previously unheard.

But another of the new technologies, two-way television, has been most frequently trumpeted as having this effect. Sometimes called "interactive television," it is a key element in a cable system called QUBE, introduced in Columbus, Ohio, by Warner Communications. Its subscribers are invited to vote or to express opinions via push buttons. Throughout the day, subscribers' views are solicited on a number of issues: they can help decide winners of talent shows, debates, or quizzes. Their reactions to candidates can be measured throughout a campaign. Enthusiasts assert that this system has finally given the voice of the people its rightful place in the political process. Others are skeptical, considering push-button participation almost a mockery of the idea of democracy, one that further reduces political discourse to pollster formulations. But public reaction has been favorable, and a number of cities have launched plans for similar systems.

In addition to push buttons, two-way systems can place a microphone and camera into the home communication center for occasional or specialized uses—ultimately, for two-way videophone and television conferences. In some cable systems a camera, automatically surveying homes, serves as burglar protection, responding to any intrusion and videotaping the intruder. While camera surveillance is cited as an exceptional benefit in discussions about the future of two-way television, it is also the basis for dire predictions. The equipment so introduced into the home, subject to activation from the outside, is precisely the means used in George Orwell's 1984 for official surveillance of citizens.

Critics further point out that systems like QUBE hold computerized demographic data on subscribing homes and that information issued from homes via push buttons, microphones, or cameras goes into the cable system's data base. In the process, an astonishing range of information about any subscriber—views, finances, associations, and comings and goings—can be on file. No matter how well this information may be protected by coded-access devices, privacy would seem to be endangered and the possibilities for authoritarian control, subtle or otherwise, greatly expanded.

INTERNATIONAL POLITICS

The conflicting tendencies discussed so far have all been examined in their implications for domestic politics. But these tendencies also have a bearing on international politics, which offers some special problems of its own. For decades, U.S. television served much of the world. Its English-language programming, dubbed into other languages, has been broadcast in many countries, dominating their media environments. Most American programming is received as "entertainment" but carries political implications all the more effectively because it is viewed as entertainment. Spy series have regularly been based on cold-war premises. Most police and other action series seem to imply that social problems are solved by the violent defeat of villains by heroes. Few problems not solved in this way seem to be featured.

U.S. programming has won this hegemony to a large extent because of its low prices. Since the cost of American programs can be recouped in the home market, they enter foreign markets with an advantage over any local product. The price charged to a foreign television system is usually a small fraction of what it would cost to produce comparable material locally. For this reason, most foreign countries do not produce filmed entertainment series. At the same time, American manufacturers or their foreign affiliates are prominent among the sponsors. American advertising agencies are active on every continent.

The political implications are subtle but far-reaching. American clothes, phrases, gestures, music, customs, and products have become a normal part of the environment on every continent. Unconscious identifications so created are a political factor not measurable by any known standard but unquestionably significant. To many viewers, what is American is not "foreign."

The extent to which exported American culture influences the United States's international relationships may be greatly augmented (or challenged) by communication satellites. The satellite began as a relay instrument, a link for television and radio networks, computer networks, and cable systems. But Arthur C. Clarke, the science-fiction writer credited with conceiving the idea of the synchronous communications satellite (one that appears to hover over a fixed location), early foresaw that its implications went far beyond the relay function. In *Holiday* magazine, in September 1959, Clarke jocularly offered ideas on "how to conquer the world without anyone noticing." He considered the means available to both the United States and the Soviet Union and pointed out that ground stations, the links between satellites and television systems, are not really necessary. The Soviet Union, for example, might put a synchronous satellite high over Asia that could reach the entire continent. If, through Soviet trade missions, it could then flood the continent with low-cost television sets designed to receive the satellite directly, ground stations could pass into disuse. The technique could also be applied to Africa and elsewhere. From the satellite would flow drama, sports, dance, newscasts, quiz programs, and variety programs—everything to enthrall nations in the way that "even ostensibly educated nations have been unable to resist." The first prize on quiz programs would always be a free trip to the Soviet Union. Before long, uncommitted nations would become committed. Which of the two superpowers first establishes such a system, wrote Clarke, "may determine whether, fifty years from now, Russian or English is the main language of mankind."[5]

What Clarke did not say was that the United States and the Soviet Union might each beam satellite programming directly to the homes of the other nation. The right to communicate to all peoples by any means available, bypassing local authority, has been a key element in U.S. policy and doctrine, justifying Radio Free Europe, Radio Liberty, and other international communications activities. Similar rights are presumably available to all major and minor powers.

The possibility of such a satellite confrontation may seem remote. Yet programming by direct broadcast satellite (DBS) is already being considered by major corporations, including Sears, Roebuck and Co., and the subject is already an issue in international debate. Will DBS prove an intercultural bridge, as is sometimes suggested, or will it raise the cold war to a new fury? Will nations start targeting one another's satellites with laser beams or other disabling devices? DBS seems to have such dramatic possibilities that it casts uncertainty over the future of all other media technologies.

CONCLUSION

Examined in diverse ways, each of the new technologies offers conflicting potentials. A resounding diffusion of information and ideas is obviously possible. But sobering possibilities for the centralization of influence and control can also be noted. The early centralizing effect of wired telegraphy and of network broadcasting will likely be repeated in other wired systems, especially in a nationwide array of systems linked by satellite. Video, alone among new technologies, seems to offer contrary possibilities.

A key ingredient in the current media explosion has been the discovery that many viewers, in spite of decades of "free" television, are prepared to pay for television programs and services and to pay premium prices for the more spectacular sports and entertainment events, as well as for such specialties as pornography. How politics will fare in this new plethora of media fare may not be clear for some time.

With cable systems offering a growing number of channels, it seems likely that the world of politics will be represented more frequently, especially on panel, interview, and debate programs. The proceedings of the House of Representatives are now carried by cable systems and occasionally prove spellbinding to some viewers. During crises, they may develop substantial audiences. The possibility thus exists that politics, more broadly present in the media mix, will become comprehensible to a growing number of people and that increased participation will be encouraged.

Yet any political program will apparently be competing at every moment with an array of sports, movies, quizzes, and variety and game shows and with reruns of situation-comedy, spy, cowboy, and police series. The new television will be a clamorous and competitive arena that may continue to downgrade the political process. It is possible that the present era, in retrospect, will be seen as one in which bread and circuses—in the form of social security and spectacular television—provided pacification and distraction while the affairs of government became increasingly mysterious and unknown.

NOTES

1. Alvin F. Harlow, *Old Wires and New Waves* (New York: Appleton-Century, 1936), p. 337.

2. Western Union, *Annual Report* (1871). quoted in *ibid.*, p. 336.

3. Harlow, p. 405.

4. Frederick Leland Rhodes, *Beginnings of Telephony* (New York: Harper, 1929), p. 397.

5. Arthur C. Clarke, "Faces From the Sky," *Holiday* (September 1959), pp. 47–48.

Erik Barnouw (left) with Satyajit Ray (center) and a reporter at the Washington, D.C., premier of *The Chess Players* at the John F. Kennedy Center for the Performing Arts. *(Author's collection)*

13

Lives of a Bengal Filmmaker: Satyajit Ray of Calcutta

THERE WAS REASON for astonishment when Satyajit Ray of Calcutta a quarter century ago won international awards with his first film, *Pather Panchali (Song of the Road)*: he had never made a film, had no experience in any branch of filmmaking, and the group working with him was almost equally innocent of experience. His cameraman had never shot a film; most of the actors had never acted. The ingredients had seemed so unpromising to distributors and other potential backers that more than twenty had rejected his proposals. Yet he finished the film, and it won wide renown and distribution.

He continued to provide surprises. In the following twenty years, often drawing on the original tyro group, he has directed twenty-five features, almost all of which have earned back their investment in his native Bengal while many also won foreign markets and honors. While he directed these films, he also wrote the screenplays, sometimes basing them on his own stories; designed scenery, costumes, and posters; in most cases composed and scored the music; served as his own director of photography; and drew animation sequences for some. To few major film artists has the term *filmmaker* been more applicable. In addition to the feature films, he has made several documentaries.

In the midst of all this filmmaking he has pursued other activities, of which his film following has been largely unaware, involving another side of his career. Since the early 1960s he has published a children's magazine for which he writes a steady stream of stories ranging from science fiction to comic detective stories—"everything I loved as a child"—which he illustrates with rollicking pictures in diverse styles. His short stories have been published in collections that have been translated from Bengali into several other Indian languages. Some of the stories have become films. The magazine was founded by his grandfather, Upendrakishore Ray, a similarly protean figure who played the violin, wrote books, painted, pioneered in half-tone block printing in India, and printed his magazine on his own press. Satyajit's father, Sukumar Ray, carried on this work, likewise drawing and writing for the magazine. His nonsense rhymes are considered children's classics; collections of them are still sold. In addition, Sukumar won recognition as "a master of the photographic art." His death when Satyajit was not yet three thrust the family into a financial crisis that led to the demise of the magazine; but after early film successes Satyajit Ray revived it and has continued to maintain it. Thus, as graphic artist, musician, writer, director, entrepreneur, Ray is a kind of Renaissance man sprung from a Renaissance family.

A question raised by this astonishing record, which has placed Ray among a select few film artists of global rank, is why it should have been achieved in a region of economic disaster, and in the midst of a film industry that has careened, spectacularly and successfully, in a quite different direction. Ray has been a notable anomaly in the Indian film world.

For some years the Indian film industry has been the world's most prolific, outranking any other country in the production of feature films. In recent years its annual output has exceeded six hundred theatrical features, more than that of Hollywood at its peak. Indians began making films at the dawn of film history, within months after a Lumière emissary demonstrated the invention in Bombay in July 1896. India had its *Train Arriving at Bombay Station* and *Poona Races 98*. The making of features began in 1912, paralleling their beginning in the United States. In the early 1920s India was outproducing Britain.

Most screen time was going to foreign films, especially from Hollywood, but Indian films were already gaining a strong hold over growing audiences. The first features were "mythologicals," about the heroes, gods, demons, and other creatures of the ancient Indian epics the *Ramayana* and the *Mahabharata*—streams of narrative that flow into all the arts of South Asia including drama, dance, song, sculpture, and painting. This factor helped Indian films reach Asian audiences far outside India, although Westerners were generally baffled by them. Other genres were added in the 1920s—"historicals" full of spectacular action, "stunt films" emulating the successes of Douglas Fairbanks, and "social films," a term that seemed to apply to almost anything in a contemporary setting.

At first glance it seemed that the advent of sound film at the end of the decade would doom the rising Indian film activity. Until that time an Indian film, with changeable subtitles to serve diverse language groups, could move throughout India and beyond. But now a film apparently had to have a specific built-in language. India's huge jigsaw puzzle of tongues—many entirely unrelated to others, precipitates of endless invasions over millennia of recorded and unrecorded time—seemed to raise impossible barriers against sound film. With the fragmentation of the market and the escalation of costs, concurrent with the world Depression, many Indian film companies collapsed and dissolved. But the language barrier also applied to foreign films. For those film companies that survived, the very first Indian sound films proved so astonishingly successful that they propelled the Indian film world into a boom atmosphere that has never quite subsided.

The first Indian sound film, *Alam Ara (Beauty of the World)*, released in 1931, included twelve songs; another film of the year had forty songs; another, sixty songs. All early sound films were saturated with music, and almost all had dances. Indian filmmakers thus opted for an "all-singing, all-dancing" rather than an "all-talking" genre. The formula removed emphasis from the spoken word and shifted it elsewhere. This was in keeping with Indian tradition—ancient Sanskrit drama had likewise featured song and dance. In fact, Sanskrit vocabulary is said to provide no way of distinguishing dance from drama. The folk theater of strolling players that had persisted through the centuries in many parts of India was likewise a song-and-dance drama. Infant Indian sound film seized on this tradition and tapped a mighty river of music, rich in associations. So successful was the formula that twenty-three years of sound-film production went by—a period that saw the release of hundreds of feature films—before an Indian producer dared to make one without songs or dances. In 1954 the filmmaker K. A. Abbas produced such a film, *Munna (The Lost Child)*. It won Western admirers and was honored at the Edinburgh Festival but failed in India, so that this reckless act of rebellion served only to buttress the reign of the formula. For the moment, formula remained king.

Song-and-dance films had their most spectacular successes in the Hindi tongue—the language having the widest reach and which the Indian founding fathers had designated as the future national language, to be given this official status after a period of preparation. The designation aroused furious campaigns of opposition, especially in the South, dominated by Dravidian languages unrelated to Hindi, which stems from Sanskrit. Yet the Hindi song-and-dance film even managed to penetrate areas where opposition was strong—suggesting to some observers that if the battle for a national tongue were ever won, it would not be through government pressure and edict but through the Hindi film-song mania. The popular obsession with film songs has continued unabated, while its music has evolved from Indian roots into an extraordinarily eclectic genre drawing on rhythms of American jazz, Latin-American music, and African music and using every conceivable instrument—from ancient Indian strings and percussion to the Victorian harmonium and the electric guitar.

The song-and-dance formula inevitably has had disastrous effects on dramatic values. It has fostered a dramaturgy in which plots are absurd and characterization simplistic and rigidly stereotyped. Its heroes, heroines, and villains live in a vacuum. The producers, by aiming for a national audience and bypassing regional concerns, have created an artificial world hardly touched by the daily troubles of most filmgoers. Its heroes and heroines seldom have visible occupations. Their dalliances may take place in splendid surroundings as remote from current life as the world of mythology. Critics complain of the "dreamworld" environment, but it holds its sway. Into an industry dominated by this tradition came Satyajit Ray.

He had his own obsessions. He wanted his characters not only to have human complexity but to be in a certain moment in a certain place in a particular web of social relationships. The "social identity" of his characters has been his constant concern. Since the social context he was most familiar with was his native Bengal, almost all his films have been made in and about Bengal. Nuances of speech, manners, gestures, clothing, decor are all essential elements of the social fabrics that fascinate him. Feeling most at home in his Bengali language, he has resisted most offers—including generous ones from Hollywood—to work in other languages, even though Bengali is understood by only some 10 percent of the people of India. His filmmaking has thus evolved into a continuous and deepening exploration of the life of one region—Bengal—yesterday and today. By the accepted wisdom of the Indian film industry, this relentless localism would doom any possibility of a wide following. Paradoxically, it is the key to Ray's international successes. It is our sense of the authentic localism that has made his work seem so "universal." Far and wide, audiences sense that the pieces fit, providing flashes of human recognition and kinship with a society that might otherwise seem only strange.

Ray's *Pather Panchali*, *Aparajito* (*The Unvanquished*), and *Apur Sansar* (*The World of Apu*) formed a trilogy that traced a family saga from the village to the city, from a remote past to yesterday, from a structured rural life to a chaotic metropolis with all its uncertainties for the future. There were probably many reasons why this epic-sized story, based on a much-admired novel that Ray had already illustrated, should have been especially meaningful to him. It held parallels to the experience of generations of the Ray family, which had its roots in rural Bengal, had known numerous reversals of fortune, and eventually had become a Calcutta family deeply enmeshed in the crises and conflicts of the modern world. The story was also a metaphor for the history of modern India.

In many ways, it foreshadowed the sweep of Ray's work during later decades. His caravansary of memorable characters has come to seem like figures in a vast landscape representing more than a century of Indian history. In exploring this landscape, Ray has sometimes focused on figures of power and privilege, and sometimes on those who willingly or unwillingly accepted domination. He has examined, from various perspectives, the microcosms surrounding the *zamindar*, as in *Jalsaghar* (*The Music Room*), 1958; the upper class husband, as in *Charulata*, 1964; the movie star, as in *Nayak* (*Hero*), 1966; the Brahman teacher, as in *Ashani Sanket* (*Distant Thunder*), 1973; the colonial commander, as in *Shatrani Ke Khilari* (*The Chess Players*), 1977; the businessman, as in several "city films," including *Aranyer Din Ratri* (*Days and Nights in the Forest*) and *Pratidwandi* (*The Adversary*), 1970.

A key aspect of Ray's handling of these figures is that he seldom makes them heroes or villains. "Villains bore me," he has said—sweeping aside much of India's film output—and for good reason. Villains are a key device for evading central problems of history. Ray, in contrast, has constantly explored the complex of devices by which establishments have legitimized and reinforced their status in ways that have secured consensus among the ruled as well as the ruling and that have often, for much of the time, eluded the consciousness of both.

Ray's handling of such matters has not endeared him to all audiences. *Shatrani Ke Khilari (The Chess Players)* is a case in point. Set in aristocratic, feudal Lucknow of 1856, it deals with the British annexation of the Kingdom of Oudh, the last quasi-independent realm of India, which was nominally ruled by Wajid Ali Shah. In keeping with the subject, the film was made partly in English and partly in Urdu, the Persianized Hindi spoken by the Lucknow ruling class. It was Ray's first film in a language other than Bengali, and was expected to give him entry to Hindi markets not usually available to him.

But characteristically, Ray saw none of the roles in hero-villain terms. His General Outram of the East India Company, the man who organizes the quiet but forceful overthrow of the King, is troubled by the illegality of his instructions, which clearly violate Britain's treaty of friendship with the King. But Outram is also a firm believer in the destiny of empire, which he expects will bring order and progress out of ancient chaos, and he regards it as his duty to history to ignore his own scruples. Besides, he considers Wajid Ali Shah an ineffectual ruler, which he is. Ray's attitude toward the King is likewise ambivalent. He depicts Wajid Ali Shah as a poet and musician of considerable accomplishment, who has no great liking for the maneuverings of statecraft and has relied on his "treaty of friendship" with the British to allow him the freedom to pursue a passion for the arts. When Britain's treachery becomes clear, he is at first determined to resist with force but finally decides to avoid shedding the blood of his people by surrendering.

Interwoven with these events are episodes involving two noblemen who have an unrestrained passion for chess. The arrangements under which the Kingdom of Oudh has been allowed to remain ostensibly independent, extracting tax revenues from its people while receiving "protection" from the British, have enabled the Oudh establishment to pursue a pleasurable life undisturbed, endlessly playing chess by ancient Indian rules, oblivious to the rougher chess being played by the British. The two nobles are trying to save their kings as their King goes under. They are even oblivious to the needs of their own wives, one of whom is dallying with her husband's nephew. Thus Ray's portrait of the fall of Oudh is a sardonic one. If it did not at once enthrall Hindi film audiences, the reasons are not obscure. Indians could not readily derive emotional satisfaction from its version of history—nor, for that matter, could the British. If there were no villains, there were no heroes either—and no action climax, such as many may have yearned for.

If there was a message, it had to do with non-involvement—with playing chess while Oudh fell. To some this message and the detailed dissection of the thrusts and maneuvers of colonialism—a dissection equally applicable to neocolonialism—seemed timely and important. Like many Ray films, it won intense admiration, but no breakthrough box office success in Hindi markets. It was, said one critic, a film "not for the heart but for the head."

To some critics the film exemplified a "detachment" characteristic of Ray, which they find irksome. They accuse him of being aloof—not "committed." If they mean that he does not enunciate doctrine, they are right. Ray is determined to leave audiences grappling with the problems and situations he has laid bare, and not to release them with formula solutions. In this respect he is perhaps more a social historian than a purveyor of popular pleasures. Yet he clearly invests his work with strong emotion, though under tight control.

That a social historian in the film medium should emerge from the turmoil and decaying splendor of Calcutta is not entirely an accident. Calcutta was the capital of British India throughout most of the era of British rule. The presence of the British government fostered the development of an Indian middle class schooled in British ways, history, literature, and values. Its more affluent families sent sons to England to be educated. All this was fostered by British policy, which aimed to develop a stratum of Indian society that would identify its interests with those of the empire. To a degree the policy succeeded, although its ultimate effect was different. The libertarian themes that run through British history and literature gradually helped to fuel the Indian independence movement, which eventually acquired an irresistible momentum.

During the nineteenth century the juxtaposition of British and Indian cultures in Calcutta under the aegis of imperial government fostered the so-called Bengal Renaissance. It dwelt in two worlds. Its

elite was steeped in the arts of the West. The joint-family homes of
many leading Indian families had their own theaters, which gradually
brought a rebirth of Indian drama, looking not to ancient Indian
models but to the drama of Europe—of Shakespeare and of Ibsen.
In all the arts a parallel process was taking place.

This ferment in the arts inevitably involved a search for identity.
And an especially significant aspect of the Bengal Renaissance was
that through the arts its practitioners rediscovered their own heritage. They took their forms from Europe but eventually focused
them on the life around them. They discovered India.

A towering figure of the Bengal Renaissance was Rabindranath
Tagore, whose spirit found expression in poetry, song, drama, essay,
dance, and painting. In the meditation center founded by his father
and that, under Rabindranath Tagore, became a university—
Santiniketan, the abode of peace, "where the world becomes one
nest"—the emphasis was on a fusion of the cultures and values of
East and West. This work made him a world figure, a Nobel Prize
winner, and in 1915 he was rewarded with a British knighthood, becoming Sir Rabindranath. But four years later he renounced the title
in protest against the Amritsar massacre—in which police, to enforce
a ban on gatherings, shot into a crowd and killed some four hundred
people. Increasingly, Tagore became a symbol of the drive for independence. Santiniketan played a significant role in the Indian redis-
covery of India. The Indian national anthem is by Tagore.

A close friend of Tagore's was Upendrakishore Ray, grandfather of
Satyajit Ray and, like Tagore, a virtuoso in several arts. Tagore visited
the Ray home often. Family theater was an activity of both families.
In the wake of the economic crisis that struck the Ray family after
the death of Satyajit's father, young Satyajit went to live with relatives while his mother taught embroidery and leather work in a home
for widows. This period of financial straits may explain why Satyajit,
when ready for college, took up the study of economics. But after
earning a B.A. in economics at the University of Calcutta in 1940 at
the age of nineteen, he went to study at Santiniketan, where he
concentrated on the graphic arts. This led to employment three years
later in the Calcutta branch of D. J. Keymer, a British advertising
agency. Four years later, at twenty-seven, he became art director of
the branch. On the side he was winning recognition as a designer of
book jackets and an illustrator of books, including an edition of the

immensely successful novel *Pather Panchali*. He was already a film devotee, choosing films according to who directed them rather than who starred in them. When he learned that a film adapted from a favorite novel was about to appear at a Calcutta theater, he sometimes wrote his own complete screenplay based on the book. Later, while watching the film, he would compare it inwardly with his own conception, noting possibilities he might have missed, as well as places where he might have done better. In the process he gained confidence in his judgment. The idea of making films was taking root.

With his friend Chidananda Das Gupta he formed—in 1947, the year of Indian independence—the Calcutta Film Society, which played a further role in his film orientation. Even more important was a lengthy visit to London for indoctrination at the D. J. Keymer head office, which gave him a chance to spend evenings at the British Film Institute, saturating himself in the works of the Italian neorealists and other European masters. Another important milestone for Ray was the arrival in Calcutta of Jean Renoir for the shooting of *The River*. Ray met him, and he and other members of the Calcutta Film Society helped Renoir search for locations. They were sometimes surprised at familiar things of Bengal that especially excited Renoir and stimulated his curiosity. In a sense, Renoir was helping Ray to discover Bengal.

Satyajit Ray, like the earlier Rays and Tagores, was a man of two cultures, colonial and Indian. But it was in keeping with the Bengal Renaissance that his obsession with the films of Western lands turned him not to imitating them but to discovering his homeland. He wanted to do for India what Roberto Rossellini had done for postwar Italy and Ingmar Bergman was doing for Sweden. When Ray began his own film work, he had little more than book knowledge of his own country, or even of his home state of West Bengal. But his films became vehicles for a twenty-five-year exploration that brought him closer and closer to his own people. Closer, at the same time, to others far away across the world. "And this," he writes, "is what amazes you most and makes you feel indebted to the cinema: this discovery that although you have roots here—in Bengal, in India— you are at the same time part of a large plan, a universal pattern. This uniqueness and this universality and the coexistence of the two, is what mainly I try to convey through my films."[1] Perhaps for the same reason, he feels no great compulsion to seek other settings. There is still so much to be learned and told about Bengal. It is a whole world.

For a time his explorations seemed lonely work. His films won early response in Bengal, but to most of India they were films in a foreign language. Their linguistic nuances made them unsuitable for dubbing; in any case, dubbing seemed to Ray an execrable practice, a corruption. In some Indian cities the films appeared with English subtitles, generally in "Sunday morning shows"—the equivalent of "art theater" showings elsewhere. Thus the Ray films appeared in most of India under precisely the same circumstances as in the United States, Germany, Japan, Mexico, China, or Australia. Most of India became aware of Ray's world fame but was only marginally familiar with his work.

Film producers of Bombay and Madras, where the bulk of the spectacular song-and-dance features are made, sometimes show pique over Ray's international celebrity. A film star ascribed it to Ray's "peddling India's poverty abroad." Bombay song-and-dance directors like to say that of course Ray's work is splendid "artistically" but that Bombay films are better "technically." The discovery that Western critics consider Ray's work superb vis-à-vis not only artistry but also technical quality—in spite of the modest budgets on which they are made—brings puzzlement and a hint of annoyance.

But Ray has also won his share of admirers in Bombay, Madras, and other film centers. Students at the Film and Television Institute of India at Pune study his work. It has become a staple in the programs of Indian film societies, which have proliferated in recent years. Stars from various sectors are eager to appear in Ray's films, even at depressed Calcutta rates, and they speak with admiration of his directing style and skills. A tall man of impressive physique, Ray directs calmly, with minimal explanations. There is an invisible wall about him, but he is unfailingly respectful to coworkers. If an actor's performance raises problems, Ray takes him quietly aside for a chat. There is very little waste of time, because every sequence has been planned in detail. Ray's scripts are littered with small sketches showing planned camera vistas; yet he can respond warmly to actor improvisations that contribute to the intended effect. Precisely to encourage such spontaneous contributions, he avoids excessive rehearsing. If an actor wants to discuss motivations, Ray is glad to do so, but he does not belabor the cast with lectures on, or analyses of, the project at hand. He invests enormous concentration in the casting process, looking ceaselessly for the right faces and voices. Because of careful planning, he uses little film, often shooting with a four-to-one ratio while other directors might use ten-to-one or even more. Most Satyajit Ray films have had budgets of less than $100,000.

A number of technicians and actors have worked with Ray repeatedly. He has no contract with any of them; they merely tend to wait until he is ready for a new production, in the hope that he will have a place for them. Partly for their sake he has moved rapidly from one production to another, always keeping a number of projects in readiness—sketching adaptations of public domain classics; writing scenarios and putting them aside; negotiating for screen rights to novels he has liked. His schedule is crowded, but he maintains an unhurried air. In the evening he likes to play the harpsichord.

When Ray began composing his own music, one highly successful Bombay film composer, Vanraj Bhatia, felt that it was an expression of ego. Ray's filmmaking, he felt, was turning increasingly into "a one-man show." But a few films later Bhatia changed his mind about Ray's music. It was a major element, he felt, in the extraordinary beauty and tautness of Ray's *Charulata*. "Few musicians in India could have given him the kind of mood music that he himself has managed to compose."[2]

Satyajit Ray has in no way affected the Indian obsession with song-and-dance films. Yet he is no longer a solitary figure. In various regions of India the work of Ray has spurred the development of "regional" styles of cinema, aiming at the fascination—and universality—of the authentically local, evoking lives at particular moments in particular places. A number of impressive younger filmmakers have emerged from this trend—Shyam Benegal, Girish Karnad, Mrinal Sen, M. S. Sathieu, B. V. Karanth, G. Aravindan. They come from various linguistic areas. They differ in many ways but share a determination to shun established formula. They too are discoverers of India. They have not shaken the film establishment but have won a following of their own. Their work has acquired the name "parallel cinema." In one way or another, it is a response to what seemed for a time a voice in the wilderness, Satyajit Ray.

Notes

1. From a documentary film on Ray by B. D. Garga, quoted in Anandam Film Society, *Montage* (July 1966).
2. Vanraj Bhatia in Anandam Film Society, *Montage* (July 1966).

Recommended Reading

Books

Barnouw, Erik, and S. Krishnaswamy. *Indian Film* 2d ed. (New York: Oxford University Press, 1980).
Bowers, Faubion. *Theatre in the East* (London: Thomas Nelson, 1956).
Das Gupta, Chidananda. *The Cinema of Satyajit Ray* (New Delhi: Vikas, 1980).
Ray, Satyajit. *Our Films, Their Films* (Bombay: Orient Longmans, 1976).
Sarkar, Kobita. *Indian Cinema Today* (New Delhi: Sterling, 1975).
Seton, Marie. *Portrait of a Director: Satyajit Ray* (Bloomington: Indiana University Press, 1971).
Wood, Robin. *The Apu Trilogy* (New York: Praeger, 1971).

Journals

Anandam Film Society. "Special Issue on Satyajit Ray." *Montage* (July 1966) Bombay.
Blue, James. "Satyajit Ray." *Film Comment* (Summer 1968) New York.
Das Gupta, Chidananada. "Ray and Tagore." *Sight and Sound* (Winter 1966–67) London.
Garga, B. D. "Historical Survey." *Seminar,* films issue (May 1960) New Delhi.
Ray, Satyajit. "Dialogue on Film." *American Film* (July–August 1978) Washington.
———. "Problems of a Bengal Film Maker." *International Film Annual* (1958) New York.

Films of Satyajit Ray

Pather Panchali (Song of the Road), 1955
Aparajito (The Unvanquished), 1956*
Paras Pathar (The Philosopher's Stone), 1957
Jalsaghar (The Music Room), 1958*
Apur Sansar (The World of Apu), 1959
Devi (Goddess), 1960
Rabindranath Tagore (documentary), 1961*
Teen Kanya (Three Daughters), 1961
Kanchanjanga, 1962
Abhijan (Expedition), 1962
Mahanagar (The Big City), 1963*
Charulata, 1964*
Two (short film for Esso World Theater), 1965
Kapurush-O-Mahpurush (The Coward and the Saint), 1965*
Nayak (Hero), 1966*
Chiriakhana (The Zoo), 1967
Goopy Gyne Bagha Byne (Goopy and Bagha), 1969
Aranyer Din Ratri (Days and Nights in the Forest), 1970*
Pratidwandi (The Adversary), 1970
Seemabadha (Company Limited), 1971*
Sikkim (documentary), 1971
Ashani Sanket (Distant Thunder), 1973
The Inner Eye (documentary), 1974
Sonar Kella (The Golden Fortress), 1974
Jana Aranya (The Middleman), 1974
Bala (documentary), 1976
Shatrani Ke Khulari (The Chess Players), 1977
Joi Baba Felunath (The Elephant God), 1978
Hirak Rajar Deshay (Kingdom of Diamonds), 1980

---

*In the Library of Congress Film Collection.

The author's brother Victor Barnouw. *(Author's collection)*

14

GAMES

CENSORSHIP in its wide sense—that is, the drawing of lines that are not to be crossed—can be discussed from many perspectives, since many kinds of people are involved in it or affected by it. I would like briefly to focus on the strange—sometimes bizarre—relationships that develop between censors and their victims—or perhaps I should say, between censors and their beneficiaries, since there are diverse views on the value of those *interventions*, as they have been called. I must confess that having worked in radio, then television, in many capacities at various levels, in fiction and nonfiction, I have felt indignant on many sides of many an altercation. But I remain fascinated by the games that are played in the process. Our media take hierarchic forms, and it seems to me that much game-playing goes on between the levels. The games are not unlike those played within family circles. It is hard to imagine family life without taboos and appeals to duty and to a sense of responsibility—themes that seem sure to pervade discussions here at Ravenna. So family life provides early training for media tussles. As future censors, we get our first sense of what we can achieve in the way of control, and what good it may do us. As future victims, we get our first practice in games of resistance. Thus our title: "Games."

My own parents took seriously their role as parents. Both were very articulate. My father, born in Holland, was a high school teacher while we lived there. He was a more versatile scholar than this may suggest. He had studied thirteen languages including six dead ones, and could discuss at length, and with great ease, the language of the Visigoths and its influence on various modern languages. But he could not possibly bring himself to discuss sex with his children. Our English mother seems to have worried about this, and tried to persuade him to do so, but he was reluctant, and so, in fact, was she. Both, you see, were well brought up, so on this matter self-censorship

Author's keynote speech on censorship, given at *Prix Italia* in Ravenna, Italy, on June 21, 1997.

set in—which, in relation to us, was equivalent to censorship. By and large, we children were left to our own devices.

There were four of us, three boys and a girl, born over a stretch of eleven years. Fortunately my brother Will, the oldest—two years ahead of me—was extremely gregarious and managed, at an early age, to pick up an astonishing amount of information, which he doled out to me in bits with a certain condescension. So we both felt well informed. I am sure our information was shot through with errors—but that seems true of education at all levels. Meanwhile Will and I had gathered that sex was a subject not discussed with parents and that there were words—really a long list of words—that one never used in their presence. Thus Will and I managed, for a number of years, to shield our parents from the rougher side of life. I could not know that this would prove fine preparation for life in the media.

I had another brother, called Victor, seven years younger than I was. He was bright and imaginative beyond the rest of us, but child-hood diseases had left him with impaired hearing, which must at times have hampered his social development. I think Mother worried about this—more than she had worried about Will and me. One year, when Victor was ten and I was seventeen and ready to go away to Princeton University (we were in the United States now) Mother said to me one day that someone must enlighten Victor on certain important matters. She said Father really ought to do it. "But you know how he is—he just won't do it." So she said I should do it. "He looks up to you. Why don't you take him for a nice long walk along Riverside Drive and explain everything." So we had our walk.

Some television directors have endless faith in the walking narra-tor. Time again you see people walking while they explain, or walking as they sell. Perhaps it makes them look more resolute. On this day I became the walking narrator. I think it may have helped me to mask the uncertainty I felt about what I was doing. But somehow, striding along Riverside Drive, I got through my prepared remarks. To all of which Victor listened with a most puzzled look. Finally he asked, "How did people find out about this?" I think I floundered a bit on that, and used the word "instinct" a few times. Then Victor said: "Maybe that's why dinosaurs became extinct—because they didn't find out about it."

I have often pondered this dialogue. Victor's question, "How did people find out about this?" was not a bad one, at least not for modern, urban America. A century earlier, in an agrarian world, there would have been less reason to ask it. If one lived on a farm with animals, daily life would provide many answers, with fine audiovisual aids. The city is not so informative. The rise of pornography might be mentioned in this connection, as a quasi-substitute. It is seldom discussed as an educational tool, yet I have no doubt some people turn to it for enlightenment.

Only a few years after my walk with Victor, I found myself in the broadcasting industry, directing programs for an advertising agency. One of my first assignments was a drama series titled *The True Story Court of Human Relations*, which was not as grand as it sounds. It consisted of stories from *True Story* magazine, which specialized in confessional tales. In a typical story a young woman tells of being seduced, then abandoned, by some fellow who proves unworthy. She, after bearing a child out of wedlock, is trying hard to put her life together again. The end was always moral, but *True Story* owed its success to making sure that its readers—later its radio listeners—first savored fully the adventure of a sinful liaison.

The radio programs, written for us by a freelance writer, were produced by the advertising agency and broadcast live from an NBC studio. The arrangement stipulated that each script must be approved before broadcast by the network's so-called "policy reader," a lady with a very decisive manner. Before the premiere the writer, and I as director, were called to NBC for a meeting with the lady. She welcomed us and said she would try to make life easy for us. "But," she warned, "don't let any of your characters set up housekeeping without benefit of clergy. That's my main concern." Our writer, who was already a radio veteran, immediately said, "No problem." I was amazed to hear him say that. Later I asked him, wasn't he aware that people doing things without benefit of clergy were *True Story*'s bread and butter? It thrived on the sinful part. The writer was unperturbed. He said there were always ways of handling such things. When I began to receive his scripts, I saw what he meant. In one of them, the sinful adventure was there all right, in full bloom. But then we learn, near the very end of the program, that there had been a secret marriage. So in retrospect all was completely kosher. If we thought it was sinful, that was only because we didn't have all the information. The NBC lady approved the script.

There were many secret marriages in our series. They were *True Story* purified. The irony was that this laundered version was broadcast to persuade people to buy the magazine and relish the "adult" version, perhaps imperiling their moral nature. The NBC lady did not worry about that. Her job was to keep the air clean.

Censorship of all sorts became more complicated in television. Angry reactions from the audience were still feared, but anger from sponsors became a more pressing worry, and they, in turn, worried increasingly about pressure groups, which were ready to threaten ruinous publicity and even boycotts. Through the fifties and sixties television was thriving but was also, increasingly, a social and cultural battleground.

I remember vividly the to-do over a play called *Thunder on Sycamore Street* by one of the most talented writers of early television, Reginald Rose. I remember also the ingenuity with which he battled the censoring interventions. The script was based on an incident in a Midwestern suburb, when a Negro couple bought a house in what had been an all-white neighborhood, and prepared to move in. Neighbors mounted a campaign to dissuade them, or else to ensure their quick departure. The script proposed that three virtually identical houses be built in the studio, side by side. Action would move from one to another. In one we would see neighbors gathering, discussing strategies against the newcomers. In the second we would meet the new family, needless to say, nice people. In the third, a man who has mixed feelings, but eventually takes a stand with the black couple. Reginald Rose was told by network, sponsor, and advertising agency that his script was brilliant. They had lavish praise for it. They were eager to broadcast it. But one small change was needed. A trivial one, they assured him. The Negro couple must be changed to "something else." Anything else. A Negro as beleaguered protagonist in a drama was out of the question for television. It would rouse all kinds of furies. Instead, it was suggested that the newcomer be an ex-convict. Wasn't vigilantism the play's real theme? To Rose the suggestion was absurd. It was not why he had written the play. However, he glimpsed in it a possible strategy. To their surprise he accepted the suggestion.

In the play that went on the air, much was familiar to the censors. There were the aroused neighbors, determined to get rid of the new family. There were the agitated arguments about falling real estate prices, the loss of investment values. And speeches like: "If we let one of them in, they'll all be coming." But—there was no mention of just what was wrong with the newcomers—whose ethnicity, by the way, was unclear. All we knew was that the neighborhood was determined to keep them out. The why was left for the audience to fill in. Since the forbidden racial issue had been eliminated, the script was approved.

Audience studies later made clear what had happened. The play had become a kind of Rorschach test, producing an inventory of audience prejudices. Each viewer apparently decided, quite quickly, what must be wrong with the newcomers. Some thought they must be communists; others, that they were probably Puerto Ricans, or Asians. When it was mentioned, near the end, that the man had been in prison, that fitted well with their assumptions. If he was a communist, of course he'd been in jail. That seemed logical. The censors in this case had tried to banish intergroup antagonisms, but had evoked a whole tangle of such antagonisms.

Through the seventies and eighties the assaults of pressure groups continued, and pushed the networks into new defensive strategies, vividly described by Kathryn Montgomery in a book titled *Target Prime Time*. The policy readers mushroomed into large entities with names like Standards and Practices Division. Instead of waiting for crises to develop, then coping with them as best they could, the network censors now tried to anticipate them, defuse them, contain them. They kept in touch with the most virulent of the pressure groups, invited them to the office, and heard their views. They even told them, in advance, about shows that might anger them. They were given scripts to read, and invited to make suggestions. Arguments that might have erupted in the public arena took place, instead, in network offices. Many disagreements remained unresolved, but acrimony seemed to wane. Asked for comment, protesters sometimes offered feasible ideas.

The series *Cagney and Lacy*, about two female police officers, put the new policy to a severe test. The producers planned an episode in which the policewomen had to track down the person who had violently attacked a clinic where abortions were performed. The clinic operated legally but was assailed on religious grounds by groups that called themselves "pro-life." Opposing them were groups calling themselves "pro-choice." The arguments swirled around network offices. The groups were determined that their own views be eloquently and forcefully presented. They were allowed to assist that process. The network worried about "balance," which became a watchword. Each side must be *equally* eloquent. For a time the network felt it essential that one of the policewomen be "pro-life" and the other "pro-choice." The producers rejected this as out of character. The network finally proposed that one of the women should have a conservative father who was strongly anti-abortion. Thus characters were invented to produce the required "balance." What took place in the network offices was a kind of shuttle diplomacy, leading to a truce, secured by a script that gradually became protest-proof. When the Prix Italia management speaks of the quest for "quality television," is this what they have in mind? I hardly think so. But I am sure much more will be said on this subject before we leave Ravenna.

I have often heard it said that any subject can be discussed in broadcasting, provided one avoids words at which people have been taught to take offense. People are less afraid of ideas, the argument runs, than of words. A sequence in my own professional life, one that riveted my attention for some years, may cast light on this.

Not far from Ravenna, in Verona, there lived five hundred years ago a poet named Fracastoro, who was also known as a physician. His poems were written in Latin. One of them, a long narrative poem, was about a shepherd, a gentle shepherd who contracted a mysterious, frightening disease. That disease eventually took its name from the poor shepherd. Because the disease seemed so intractable, its very name came to inspire dread. Five centuries later that was still true. In the 1930s, in the United States, most newspapers would not print the word. Anyone in radio or television—which was just beginning—knew that this word must not go out on the air or something terrible would happen. The Hollywood Code banned the whole subject. It was as though the word itself were thought to transmit the infection. Then a U.S. Surgeon General, Dr. Thomas Parran, head of the U.S. Public Health Service, began to denounce this self-censorship. He said, "We could probably wipe this disease out completely, but only if we can talk about it." *Time* magazine praised his stance and put Dr. Parran's picture on the cover of the magazine—always an important tribute. At that time *Time* magazine was represented on radio by a series called *The March of Time*, forerunner of the more famous film series. *Time* decided to devote a sequence on the radio series to Dr. Parran and his cause. The network at first rejected this idea but, on further thought, decided it would be all right, provided the disease was not mentioned by name. And so a rather bizarre broadcast took place, dramatizing laboratory struggles, then ending with a narration along these lines: "And so the struggle continues against this age-old scourge, this dreaded disease, that by a strange irony is named after a shepherd in a Latin poem, a shepherd whose name was Syphilus."

A few years later I acquired a role in this strange cause. To my office at Columbia University came a visitor from the U.S. Public Health Service, who said he represented its venereal disease division. Then he said: "We have a problem, in which we think you can help us." I couldn't imagine how that could be, but was ready to listen. He then explained that the American Congress had approved, and voted to fund, a massive campaign to find—and treat—the more than three million people in the United States who were believed to have syphilis without knowing it. This situation had come about, he explained, because of the tricky pattern of syphilis. Its early symptoms, such as a sore and a rash, always go away of their own accord, with or without treatment. This encourages self-medication, and of course plays into the hands of quacks. Many a patient is sure he is well, when the disease may only have gone into hiding, entering a long latent period that may last ten or twenty years, during which only a bloodtest can show the infection. But if not treated, he or she becomes a candidate for the final destructive phase of syphilis, which may bring blindness, paralysis, or insanity, depending on where the germ has lodged. It may also bring death.

My visitor explained that the American government was spending, at the time of his visit, some $20 million a year maintaining the syphilitic blind and insane in public institutions, and the cost kept going up. "Now this," he said, "makes no sense whatever"—because three years earlier, in 1943, a doctor stationed on Staten Island experimentally treated four syphilis patients, men in the armed forces, with penicillin, and a week later found all to be cured, completely. Bloodtests showed no sign of the disease. The horrors of late syphilis no longer loomed over them. All could go back to normal lives, raise families, earn a living, and pay taxes. The same was true of the elusive three million, if they could be found and treated. That was the aim of the coming plan, which had won congressional support on a strict dollars-and-sense basis.

My visitor explained its procedure. Some non-profit group—

perhaps we at Columbia—would be commissioned to produce a package of recorded programs, for radio and perhaps television, designed to make known the pattern of this disease, so that any listener who had reason to suspect that he might be one of the three million could come in for a blood test, and treatment if needed. Treatment would be free. The programs would be scheduled in any city or state that wanted such a drive in its jurisdiction. "Of course we know," said our visitor, "that most media now ban the use of the word. That may prove a problem. But the broadcast media are meant to serve the public interest, convenience, and necessity, which may perhaps give them a special obligation in the matter—more than other media. How do you feel about that?" he asked. I answered, "Sounds fine to me."

It came to pass that Columbia University, in competitive bidding, won the contract to produce the programs. The emphasis was on radio, but other media were included. The materials were first used in Tennessee and then in all other states except Maine, which said it had no syphilis problem. The campaign proved endlessly interesting. How does one gain the attention of people who have syphilis without knowing it? How does one get them to act? What genres of programming would one turn to? For those who would like the details, I have reviewed the whole story in my *Media Marathon*, published last year. In the context of the present discussion, it may hold interest because in this case the U.S. government was intervening not to censor, but to prevent censorship by others. Let me also say a word about results. The Tennessee Health Department reported that in 1949, 18,032 syphilis cases were brought to treatment through radio, in that state alone. Since all these people were asked to name, if they could, which radio program had brought them, we acquired invaluable information on which to base further programs. Results in many parts of the country were similar. By 1952 Columbia's School of Medicine reported that it was becoming difficult to find cases of late syphilis to demonstrate to medical students. By the end of that decade syphilis was no longer in the spotlight. It was overshadowed by a new epidemic, AIDS, for which syphilis seemed merely a rehearsal.

One of the most unusual items in our campaign was a short recording that we produced with an eye to the nation's jukeboxes. It was a ballad titled "That Ignorant Cowboy." I wrote the words; the music was composed and sung by folksinger Tom Glazer, with a cowboy chorus for the refrain. Produced at Columbia University, it was taken over for commercial distribution by Mercury Records, and won the support of the Music Operators of America, the association of jukebox operators. It was also introduced to a nationwide audience over the ABC network by the noted conductor Paul Whiteman. "That Ignorant Cowboy" was condemned by cowboy Gene Autry, who said cowboys are not ignorant, but the Surgeon General gave it warm support. In some cities local censorship discouraged its distribution. In others, such as San Francisco, the jukeboxes wore out many copies of the disk. "That Ignorant Cowboy" traces, step by step, the evolution of a typical syphilis case. I like to think of our cowboy as a cultural successor to Fracastoro's hapless shepherd. Here now is the cowboy.

"That Ignorant Cowboy"

An ignorant cowboy went out on a spree
And oh what an ignorant cowhand was he!
He had a few drinks and his head was awhirl
And he ended up in the arms of a girl
        Called Katey!
That ignorant cowboy, that ignorant, ignorant cowboy!

Now that cowboy was awfully handsome, they say,
As I'm sure he could tell from his mirror each day,
But many weeks later one morning he saw
A rash on his face, and he cried with a roar
        "What is it?"
That ignorant cowboy, that ignorant, ignorant cowboy!

That cowboy was worried and fretted and frowned
And he went to his medicine chest and he found
Some wonderful tonic that must have been hot
Supposed to be good for whatever you got
        And he took it!
That ignorant cowboy, that ignorant, ignorant cowboy!

Now that cowboy each morning he washed at the sink,
And then came one morning when what do you think?
The spots on his face they had all gone away
He looked and he shouted, "Ti-yippi-ti-yay!
        I'm cured!"
That ignorant cowboy, that ignorant, ignorant cowboy!

That handsome young cowboy was happy once more,
'Cause nobody ever had told him the score,
But the germ that had got him was still there inside,
'Cause this is a treacherous germ that will hide
                    Inside
An ignorant cowboy, an ignorant, ignorant cowboy!

Now pardners, it surely is sorrowful strange
To think of that cowboy a-riding the range
Not knowing some day he'll be surely struck down
By the germ that he caught when he went up to town
                    On a spree!
That ignorant cowboy, that ignorant, ignorant cowboy!

A ranch on the range isn't likely to find
Much use for a cowboy who's dead, lame, or blind,
So if you've known Katey please listen to this,
Only a doctor can cure sy-phi-lis!
                    Don't be
An ignorant cowboy, an ignorant, ignorant cowboy!

Erik Barnouw and his first wife, Dotty, who "introduced the doggie bag" into the Soviet Union. *(Author's collection)*

15
Introducing the Doggie Bag into the Soviet Union

SOME EVENTS are trivial in themselves but become unshakable memories. For me, such an event took place in Moscow in 1972 when my first wife, Dotty, introduced the doggie bag into the Soviet Union. We were at one of Moscow's better restaurants, the Georgian Restaurant, with a documentary filmmaker whom I was to interview for my book *Documentary*. The lunch, starting with an enormous soup, had been plentiful. In the middle of the table the waiter had placed two long loaves of Georgia bread. Dotty had eaten a chunk from one of them and pronounced it delicious; the other loaf remained intact. Eyeing it, Dotty commented that in the U.S. in such a situation, she would ask for a doggie bag. The Russian filmmaker was baffled by the remark. Dotty explained that it was a conventional deception; one yearns to have the bread but pretends it's for a dog. The Russian was entranced by this glimpse into U.S. culture. He called the headwaiter, and they engaged in urgent colloquy. The headwaiter left, returning with a newspaper. Wrapping the untouched loaf in it, he presented it with a bow to Dotty. That evening, in our hotel room, we supped on Georgia bread, cheese and wine while watching Moscow television—which, astonishingly, showed us our classmate Jacob Beam, who had become U.S. ambassador to the U.S.S.R. He was at Moscow's airport to greet President Richard Nixon as the latter arrived for the Moscow Summit of 1972—an interval in the Watergate imbroglio. We were spellbound. Supper was delicious.

16

The Kaufman Saga:
A Cold War Idyll

In 1971–72 I visited film archives and studios in twenty countries in preparation for a history of the documentary film. My wife, Dotty, went with me; together we viewed over seven hundred films. As we approached Moscow I felt nervous. Letters I had sent four months earlier to its archive, documentary film studio and film makers' association had all gone unanswered. What did this mean? Would our Moscow research plans go down the drain? Then in Belgrade—last stop before Moscow—a letter from the U.S.S.R. awaited us. My letters had apparently converged at some point of authority where a decision could be made. I was given a phone number to call on our arrival.

The number led me to one Bella Epstein, a dynamic lady and zealous film devotee. At Dom Kino, the House of Film, she explained in rapid Russian-accented English: "This is the headquarters of the Association of Film Makers. A screening room is reserved for you each morning. My task is to get you the films you want to see, and arrange appointments. I did not know if you knew Russian; I assumed you did not, so I have arranged for a high school English teacher, Sonya Berkovskaya, to be released from her teaching duties during your stay, to translate for you."

Astonishingly, this routine began the following morning, with films from a wish-list I had sent with my letters. The list began with films of Vertov (Denis Kaufman) and his brother Mikhail Kaufman, Vertov's main cameraman and the central character in their most famous film, *The Man with the Movie Camera*—which was available in the United States and was shown annually at Columbia University. Many of their other films had not been available, including some episodes of their *Kino Pravda*, newsreels of 1922–25, and films made by Mikhail Kaufman without Vertov.

I discussed with Bella my special interest in the Kaufman brothers.

The eldest, Denis—who had renamed himself Dziga Vertov during the 1917 revolution (both names suggesting a rapid whirling motion perhaps symbolizing a spinning film reel—or revolution itself)—was known as "father of the documentary" in Russia, as Robert Flaherty was known in the United States. Their careers had striking parallels. Each had taken up film during the 1910s. After a brief period of prominence in the early 1920s, each had worked for the rest of his life on the fringes of his nation's film industry, which preferred dream films. Both continued their missionary struggle for a new kind of film, one not built on studio artifice. Both hated large production units. Both died in the early 1950s. Each was survived by the wife and brother who had been his chief collaborators, who then carried on the mission. Their genre lived and grew in importance. Flaherty's work inspired a generation of non-studio films including ethnographic films, while Vertov's *Kino Pravda* was said to have inspired *The March of Time* as well as the *cinéma vérité* movement named after the Vertov newsreel.

I had become well acquainted with Frances Flaherty, Robert's widow, and with David Flaherty, his brother, and had learned a good deal about early documentary history from them. I hoped in Moscow to learn more about Vertov's career and impact. If Mikhail Kaufman and Elizaveta Svilova, Vertov's widow, were alive, I hoped to interview them. And there was something else. In 1954 one Boris Kaufman, a war refugee from France, had scored an impressive success in the United States as cameraman for *On the Waterfront* and later for other films including *Baby Doll* and *Twelve Angry Men*. He too was said to be a brother of Vertov. Was this true? Some seemed to doubt it. In France, Boris Kaufman had worked with the French director Jean Vigo on *A Propos de Nice*, one of the "city films" of the 1920s. In a monograph on Vigo published in 1971, the film historian Sales Gomes had described Boris Kaufman as "a cameraman of Russian origin" and had then speculated: "Boris is often confused with Mikhail Kaufman, Dziga Vertov's brother and cameraman on the most important of the *Kino Pravda* films. Boris is perhaps the third Kaufman brother, the youngest, but it is also possible that Vigo and Boris deliberately created a myth."[1]

I told Bella I hoped to sort all this out. She said she could tell me nothing about Boris, and did not know Svilova's whereabouts. But she knew that Mikhail was alive. For years he, like Vertov, had lived under a cloud of official disfavor. But a rehabilitation seemed to be in process, and it was now possible to mention both of them and even to speak well of them. Bella was clearly an admirer of Mikhail and seemed anxious to arrange an interview.

Each morning at the screening room a pile of film cans awaited us, brought overnight from the archive outside Moscow. At the screenings the young Sonya Berkovskaya, our attractive red-headed schoolteacher, sat between Dotty and me and did simultaneous translation—as she did regularly for the Moscow film festivals. At some time during each morning Bella was likely to pop into the screening room with an excited announcement such as, "We're lunching with Grigori Chukrai!" or "We will meet with Roman Karmen!" On the third morning she was more excited than usual. Mikhail Kaufman would come for an interview that afternoon.

Thus began a strange, memorable sequence. We conversed in a quiet Dom Kino lounge, drinking tea. On this occasion Bella herself did the translating, as well as tea-pouring. I had my tape recorder running. She treated Mikhail Kaufman with deep respect, as some patriarchal leader. He had a courtly manner. In his mid-seventies, he seemed in good health but spoke slowly, with a quiet, resonant voice. I had questions ready, but Kaufman forestalled these with an urgent question of his own. The following discussion, stretched out via Bella's translations, unwound slowly.

"Mr. Kaufman says he is worried about Boris. Do you know whether Boris is all right? He has not heard from Boris for several months."

"I don't know Boris. I've never met him. You mean they write to each other?"

"Mr. Kaufman says he writes to Boris often, and Boris writes to him."

"You mean regularly?"

"He says they write regularly."

"Do letters go through without difficulty?"

After Bella relayed this question, he considered before replying. Then Bella reported: "Mr. Kaufman thinks they are often read by others. There are delays. Usually the letters arrive."

"When did they last see each other?"

"1917."

"All this time, letters have gone back and forth?"

"Yes."

"What would they write about?"

Hearing this question translated, Mikhail Kaufman smiled reminiscently. "I taught him cinematography by mail."

A saga gradually emerged. The Kaufman family originally lived in Bialystok, in the Polish part of the Czarist empire. The parents were both librarians. When the Great War erupted in 1914, they decided to take their sons eastward to what seemed the comparative safety of Moscow. Denis pursued advanced studies. But in 1917 he and Mikhail were quickly caught up in the excitement of the Revolution. Denis volunteered to the cinema committee and became Dziga Vertov. During the years of foreign intervention and civil war (1917–20) he helped to make agitprop films to further the Soviet cause. The parents meanwhile decided to take the much younger Boris back to Poland, away from the turmoil. When peace came to Europe, they sent him on to France for his education. In the young Soviet Union Vertov had become a writer of zealous manifestos, calling on film artists to play a formative role in shaping the new order—not with dream films but with films of "Soviet actuality." The idea won support from a high source—Lenin. In 1922 Vertov, now joined by Mikhail, was able to launch a new kind of newsreel—*Kino Pravda*, or *Film Truth*—with Mikhail as chief cameraman and Svilova as editor.

Mikhail, with my tape recorder running, recalled this period through a mist of nostalgia. They worked ceaselessly. Vertov would outline larger strategies, then send Mikhail and other cameramen out into the world to record events of the hour: the moment when a Moscow tramline, long out of operation in torn-up streets, began running again; army tanks, used as tractors, leveling an area for an airport; a hospital trying to salvage, with minimal means, child drifters surviving in rubble. *Kino Pravda*–cameramen abhorred staged action: they caught moments in market-places, factories, schools, taverns, streets—glimpses of order emerging from chaos. Mikhail recalled that he never thought of it as work; it seemed a life necessity, like eating or breathing. When he approached exhaustion and was ordered by Vertov to the country for a rest, he found himself unable to enjoy the beauty around him. "When I could not see it with the help of my camera, it was not beauty for me."

At Svilova's editing tables, under Vertov's supervision, accumulating footage began also to be made into feature-length documentaries, like *One Sixth of the World*, which was widely shown abroad, especially in cineclubs. Boris saw it in Paris.

After the death of the elder Kaufmans, Mikhail felt a special responsibility for the faraway Boris. He wrote him regularly, telling about the film work. Boris was drawn into similar work, making film studies of the Seine and the Champs Elysées. His cinematography impressed the cineaste Jean Vigo, who enlisted him for *A Propos de Nice*, which was made as a Vigo-Kaufman co-production. While it established Boris as a documentary producer, it was his camera work that became the key to much of his later career, in France and elsewhere. When World War II broke out, Boris became a war refugee once again and embarked for Canada, where he found work as a cameraman for the National Film Board of Canada, organized by John Grierson. Later Boris entered the United States, became a U.S. citizen, and began a film career there.

It seemed extraordinary to me that the mail link had persisted through war and Cold War, including the blacklist years in the United States, when some studios and networks had asked their workers for non-communist affidavits and loyalty oaths. In Russia, I assumed, the atmosphere had been at least as oppressive and probably more so. I asked if Mikhail had ever, during those years, talked with Boris by phone. Mikhail shook his head as if to indicate it would have been unthinkable.

Mikhail wanted us especially to see two of his own films, made after the conclusion of the *Kino Pravda* series. One was *Moscow*, made with Ilya Kopalin in 1927—one of the international wave of "city films." The other was *In Spring*, made in 1939—a feature-length film shown abroad but always in such mutilated form that he wanted us to see the original. He explained that it depicted the destructive violence of spring storms and floods, and then the glory of new birth. Mikhail had used all this as a metaphor for revolution, which seemed to him inevitably violent in the cleaning out of the old—the logjam of entrenched bureaucracies and hierarchies—but also essential in setting the stage for rebirth. Unfortunately, said Mikhail, foreign distributors had removed all the symbolic content and presented the work as a glorious nature film.

I sent an overnight cable to my colleague Stefan Sharff at Columbia University, inquiring about Boris. It seemed to me likely that Sharff, being Polish and a cameraman, would know Boris Kaufman or know where to find him. A reply came promptly. At the next meeting with Mikhail over a long lunch, I was able to tell him that Boris was fine but worried about Mikhail, having had no word from him for several months. It seemed to be a time for mail delays. Was there a special reason? The Nixon-Brezhnev summit taking place at that time? We would never know.

Dotty and I assumed from the beginning of our visit that the task assigned to Bella—and perhaps to Sonya—was not only to serve us but to watch us, and probably to report on our activities. This did not trouble us. During a week's research and interviews in Hollywood at the Universal Pictures lot—for the book *The Image Empire*—the same procedure was followed: a charming girl assigned by management was our constant companion and intermediary. The same procedure had been followed at CBS News in New York, during similar research at the huge block of offices and studios on West 57th Street. It seemed a sensible merging of "public relations" and "security" functions. But it created cautious relationships. We enjoyed the company of Bella and Sonya but stuck to the business at hand. We avoided politics.

Mikhail gave me photos reproduced from his family album. There was one I found especially haunting. It was from the Bialystok days, and showed the three brothers together. The two older boys were in school uniforms. Boris looked childlike beside them. The photo eventually appeared in my book *Documentary: A History of the Non-Fiction Film* (New York: Oxford, 1974).

Back at Columbia, I learned that Boris Kaufman lived on 9th Street in downtown New York. His wife answered my phone call. I said I was anxious to interview Boris and mentioned that I had been in Moscow and seen Mikhail, and wanted to tell Boris about it. Could she suggest a convenient time? She seemed on guard. It was as though she sensed I might be a KGB agent, planning something devious or dangerous. She promised to call me back but no call came. A few days later I tried again and once more found her edgy and evasive. On my third try, Boris answered. He too seemed wary but I persisted, and he finally set a time for a visit. This took place in his living room, with Mrs. Kaufman watching from an adjoining room through the open door. I set up my recorder. Boris was brief in reply to my questions, but we managed to clarify several points in his career. In the United States his main achievement had been as cinematographer for feature films. He became a specialist in features shot on location, like *On the Waterfront*, which Hollywood tended to call "documentaries." In a sense they did represent, for Boris, a continuation of his documentary beginnings. One comment in the interview, concerning Mikhail, especially fascinated me. Boris said: "Mikhail taught me cinematography by mail."

After the interview I brought out my cassette of the Mikhail interview. I asked Boris if he would like to hear his brother's voice. Without waiting for a reply I started the record. Boris continued to look uneasy for a while, but soon a change came over him. He listened with growing intensity, sometimes with astonishment. As Mikhail talked about his work and the mysteries of the film medium, Boris kept exclaiming: "Our ideas are so similar! So similar!" It was clearly an emotional experience. Later I sent Boris a copy of the photo from Mikhail's album. He wrote back: "Thank you very much for the photo of the three of us. I didn't have it but somehow remember it. It's not easy to face oneself through time, telescoping into the past. It brings back images, sounds, even odours."

To me the unfolding Kaufman saga was a wondrous story. I mentioned it to friends at the Museum of Modern Art, who at once conceived the idea of a MOMA exhibition of "Films of the Kaufman Brothers." It seemed a splendid idea for a major retrospective series. Weeks later I inquired how the plan was progressing, and learned that it had been quickly abandoned. Boris had said: "No! Absolutely not!" He was very decisive about it. "I have nothing to do with all that!" he said. It seemed to me, sadly, that I was hearing a kind of loyalty oath.

NOTES

1. Sales Gomes, P.E., *Jean Vigo* (Berkeley: University of California Press, 1971).

INDEX